Ideology and the Urban Crisis

SUNY Series in Urban Public Policy
Mark Schneider and Richard Rich, Editors

Ideology and the Urban Crisis

Peter J. Steinberger

STATE UNIVERSITY OF NEW YORK PRESS
ALBANY

Published by
State University of New York Press, Albany

● 1985 State University of New York

All rights reserved

Printed in the United States of America

No part of this book may be used or reproduced
in any manner whatsoever without written permission
except in the case of brief quotations embodied in
critical articles and reviews.

For information, address State University of New York
Press, State University Plaza, Albany, N.Y., 12246

Library of Congress Cataloging in Publication Data

Steinberger, Peter J., 1948-
    Ideology and the urban crisis.

    (SUNY series on urban public policy)
    Bibliography: p. 163
    Includes index.
    1. Urban policy. 2. Ideology. I. Title. II. Series.
JS91.S73 1984   320.8   84-8637
ISBN 0-87395-956-6
ISBN 0-87395-957-4 (pbk.)

                          10 9 8 7 6 5 4 3 2

CONTENTS

Preface	vii
1. Ideology and the Urban Crisis	1
2. The Managerial Mood	26
3. Community and Participation	63
4. Possessive-Individualism	99
5. Toward a Philosophy of Urban Politics	128
Notes	151
References	163
Index	171

PREFACE

This book is intended primarily for students of urban politics who are interested in normative questions but who have no systematic background in political philosophy. During the past fifteen years or so, a large literature has emerged which treats the crisis of the cities from a perspective that might be variously termed normative, prescriptive, or ideological. This literature includes treatises on urban planning, exercises in public choice theory, populist and Marxist analyses, essays on urban reform, and the like. Some of these writings have earned considerable attention and even notoriety. But the unfortunate bifurcation of much graduate education in social and political science has left many urbanists unconfident in dealing with such materials. My goal, therefore, has been to organize the normative literature so as to make it more comprehensible and to provide a basis for its intelligent criticism.

The book is also intended for political philosophers who have a serious though secondary interest in urban problems. I would hope to have provided them with a novel synthesis of normative urban theory and a distinctive critique of the normative materials. I would hope further to have described some of the requirements of a more satisfying philosophy of urban politics.

My aims are thus rather modest. The chapters that follow report no new findings regarding the urban crisis and no startling interpretations in political philosophy. I have simply sought to read the major normative theories of city politics in the light of certain important traditions of political thought. In the process, I have overlooked many of the empirical complexities of the urban crisis and have offered occasionally one-sided readings of difficult philosophical texts; I have done so in the interest of providing—to the extent possible—a synthesis that is at once accurate, accessible, and concise.

For example, I have assumed without argument that there is indeed an urban crisis. Many would disagree with this, but to have made the argument against them would have required a very different kind of book. Moreover, the analyses that do appear here are largely unaffected by the issue of whether or not there is a crisis; indeed, the book might have been more accurately, if less dramatically, entitled *Ideology and Urban Politics*.

Similarly, though far more seriously, at numerous points complex problems in political philosophy have been ignored, circumvented, or even dangerously oversimplified. But to have given a full account of, say, Hobbes's theory of obligation or the debate in ethics over utilitarianism or the foundations of natural rights theory would have required a book many times longer than the present one and would have taken the discussion very far indeed from the realities of the urban crisis. Still, I am hopeful that the analyses provided are, as far as they go, faithful to the basic themes of the texts in question.

My main arguments arise out of a certain dissatisfaction with conventional references to ideologies of urban politics. It is common to classify such ideologies as being either neoconservative, reformist, or radical. Such a division, obviously useful for some purposes, is simply not very helpful in dealing with the urban-oriented materials. For example, Robert Nisbet is typically and correctly thought to be a neoconservative. Yet the import of his work for the urban crisis—with its emphasis on alienation and community—is deeply incompatible with that of another neoconservative, Edward Banfield, for whom problems such as alienation can play no major role in any sensible discussion of urban policy. The writings of a third neoconservative, Hadley Arkes, emphasize the peculiarly ethical dimensions of city politics and are, again, largely unrelated to the concerns of Nisbet and Banfield. Thus, the category "neoconservative" turns out not to mean very much when applied to the urban crisis. If anything, the so-called reformist and radical approaches are even more diffuse and incoherent.

The typology upon which the present book is based—managerialism, communalism, and possessive individualism—

cuts across the more conventional view. It classifies approaches less in terms of manifest attitudes and recommendations than in terms of underlying theoretical presuppositions. There are, no doubt, problems with this taxonomy and some may feel that I have exaggerated differences and minimized similarities. Nonetheless, my scheme is offered in the belief that it is more responsive to what is truly important in the urban literature and provides a better basis for understanding controversies concerning urban politics and policy.

This book was written with the generous support of Reed College and the Andrew W. Mellon Foundation. Emmett Buell and Lewis Anthony Dexter, among others, provided encouragement at an early stage of the project. Charles Adrian helped me get at least some of my facts straight; but I am indebted to him for much else besides. Four anonymous reviewers read the entire manuscript for SUNY Press and provided helpful comments. To all of these individuals and institutions I am most grateful. I also owe a debt of a rather different kind to Thomas P. Jenkin, late of the University of California at Riverside.

1. IDEOLOGY AND THE URBAN CRISIS

The urban crisis—discovered in the mid-1960s, dismissed as a myth in the early 1970s—has reemerged as a central fact of American life. Fiscal insolvency, rising crime rates, white flight, environmental decay, chaos in education—such factors contribute to the atmosphere of crisis that surrounds the governance of many of our major cities. If at times the crisis image has been used too indiscriminately, we can nonetheless stipulate that much of urban America is currently plagued by conditions which do indeed threaten the good health and essential welfare of society.

Conditions such as these prompt people to think, and to articulate their thoughts in a coherent, systematic fashion. Indeed, those who study urban affairs have thought a great deal about the urban crisis, and have done so in a number of identifiable ways. The purpose of this book is to look at some of those ways, focusing in particular on "normative writings" which seek to *evaluate* and *prescribe* methods of urban governance.

My task in part is simply to survey the field, to provide a brief inventory of books and essays that approach the urban crisis from one or another ideological perspective. My deeper purpose, though, is to look critically at such perspectives and to uncover and assess the underlying philosophies upon which they are based. This is a crucial task. For the arguments of social critics and social visionaries invariably reflect deep-seated assumptions about right and wrong and about the way in which the world operates. Such assumptions are rarely made explicit, yet their influence on ideological thinking is absolutely decisive. My goal, therefore, is to understand urban ideologies by revealing their various moral and epistemological roots.

In doing so, it is hoped that some light can be shed on the urban crisis itself. To be sure, this book is in a sense just another exercise in "ideology," a treatise in the history of ideas, hence not immediately concerned with empirical reality. But when confronting a reality that plagues us and seems intractable, ideas are really all we have. Our solutions to difficult problems can only be intellectual solutions, solutions that we have *thought up*. Thus, if our thinking is somehow flawed—if our ideas make no sense, are based on implausible premises, fail the tests of logic and rationality—then our solutions can probably be no better. To make headway against the ills of our cities requires an intellectual orientation that stands up to criticism and that emerges as a view which we can judge to be both plausible and persuasive.

POLITICAL SCIENCE AND THE CITY

Since the 1920s, political scientists have eagerly sought to make their discipline truly scientific. Indeed, the so-called behavioral persuasion has come to dominate scholarship and research in most areas of American political inquiry. The consequences of this have been significant. Proponents of behavioralism can now claim, with much justification, that our knowledge and understanding of the political world has increased considerably. The application of scientific methods to the study of politics has, in particular, yielded a great deal of useful information regarding the political opinions and activities of American citizens. Beyond this, behavioralists have also been responsible for expanding our theoretical or explanatory knowledge of politics, i.e., our knowledge about *why* individuals behave the way they do. To be sure, genuine achievements in this latter respect have been much harder to come by; nonetheless, we can certainly credit behavioralists with advancing and supporting a number of genuinely provocative and original hypotheses concerning political behavior. By 1961 one of the foremost behavioralists could reasonably write at length of the behavioral movement as a major intellectual success, a successful revolution.[1]

One unfortunate consequence of the behavioral revolution, however, has been the bifurcation of political science and political philosophy. In brief, political "scientists" seek to analyze politics by relying on tools and methods borrowed from the natural sciences. They identify themselves as impartial observers who test hypotheses by gathering and manipulating discrete bits of empirical data. Political "philosophers," on the other hand, rely on a conceptual apparatus derived from the history of political thought. Their concern is with the rational meaning of the state and associated concepts; and this concern naturally leads to a preoccupation with *normative* questions, i.e., questions of values and morals. It may be that the differences between these two modes of inquiry have been exaggerated, especially by those who have periodically proclaimed the demise of political philosophy.[2] Nonetheless, the fact remains that a certain persistent division of labor does tend to characterize the academic study of politics. Behavioralists frequently undertake their investigations without adequately consulting the philosophic texts; and normative theorists are too often guilty of ignoring the empirical findings of social science. That this bifurcation need not persist is widely believed; rarely, however, is anything done about it.[3]

The split between political science and political philosophy seems to have especially plagued the study of urban politics. Curiously, the behavioral persuasion did not really come to dominate urban political science until rather late in the game. In fact, as late as 1957 Laurence J.R. Herson could lament in a famous article the lack of scientific, behavioral research into urban problems and politics. Herson argued in part that urbanists had been excessively concerned with normative questions and that these concerns had contaminated existing empirical studies. He wished to see urban politics approached from a behavioral viewpoint, one that focused on actual political activity and that utilized scientific, value-neutral research techniques.[4]

To a great extent, Herson's complaint was justified. With a few notable exceptions, urbanists tended to be primarily concerned with describing and reforming, rather than systematically explaining, the urban political process. Indeed, it was not until 1955 that the first behaviorally oriented urban textbook was published.[5] The systematic study of individual voting in American cities began in earnest only in the late 1950s.⁶ And it was around the same time that American political scientists first undertook to study in depth the power and decision-making processes of large cities.⁷

However, the conversion of urban political science to behavioralism, when it finally came about, was abrupt and nearly complete. As if consciously taking up Herson's call, urbanists began to devote themselves almost exclusively to the scientific study of city politics. While much of this new research was devoted to the analysis of particular public policies, a significant portion was also aimed at developing and testing empirical *theories* of urban politics, focusing largely, though not exclusively, on the question of community power. Edward Banfield's important study of Chicago politics was followed up by Robert Dahl and his students whose research on New Haven was, in turn, supported or criticized by a host of studies, all of them of course empirical in orientation.⁸ Other researchers extended our knowledge about political participation in urban areas, generally focusing on urbanization itself as a causal factor.⁹ Still others examined variations in the structure of city governments, explaining them or their consequences with reference to the demographic and/or cultural characteristics of urban areas.¹⁰ And finally, an emergent school of thought, loosely derived from the human ecology tradition of sociology, sought to develop an empirical theory of urban political behavior based on spatial factors.¹¹ Indeed, it is clear that by the late 1960s Herson's lament was genuinely obsolete: urban political science had become overwhelmingly "behavioral."

But the behavioral revolution tended to supplant, not merely supplement, the normative approach to urban politics. This is not to say that normative theorizing about the city ceased altogether. It is to say, however, that prescriptive writing was, for a period of several years, very nearly invisible. The precise reasons for this can only be guessed at. Scholars who might otherwise have devoted themselves to normative or philosophic research may well have turned their energies instead to empirical/scientific investigations. Those writers who did persist in their normative concerns may have simply been ignored by colleagues preoccupied with gathering data and testing hypotheses. More generally, we can point to the obvious attractiveness of an urban political science for specialists eager to catch up with the rest of the discipline. Indeed, this attractiveness was enhanced by the fact that urban political systems could be fruitfully considered microcosms of political systems in general—manageable, researchable, relatively isolated units in which the essential processes of all politics could be identified and documented.[12] In any case, the study of urban affairs was, for a number of years, bereft of the kind of normative discourse which is, I would suggest, the lifeblood of any systematic inquiry into politics.

It is an essential premise of this book that there has once again been a significant shift in urban-oriented political science, a partial turning away from behavioralism and a rediscovery of normative questions. In the past decade and a half, the study of urban politics has once again recaptured something of its prescriptive focus. The problem of how cities *should* be governed has regained its place in importance beside the question of how they actually are governed. Numerous monographs and articles have been written offering solutions to our cities' problems. These writings are widely discussed. They have generated a good deal of controversy, raising questions about the purposes of urban government, influencing federal policies toward the city, and generating in the process a large volume of related empirical research. If Herson's "lost world" has long since been discovered and surveyed, then we may suggest that the normative contexts of that world, its moral and intellectual contexts, are now being delineated and assessed.

This resurgence of normative thinking about urban politics is attributable to a variety of factors including intellectual, historical, and political factors. Intellectually, one must point above all to the declining authority of behavioralism in American political science. Again, the predominance of behavioralism is utterly beyond dispute. Nonetheless, its claim to exclusivity began to wither somewhat under a steady barrage of attacks during the 1960s. These attacks took a variety of forms. One argument concerned the degree to which the procedures of the physical sciences could be appropriate for understanding social and political phenomena.

Critics of behavioralism, relying on the interpretive or hermeneutic lessons of Dilthey, Weber, and Schutz, argued that human or social facts could not be reasonably reduced to mere physical and quantifiable bits of data and, therefore, could only be comprehended through a variety of empathetic techniques associated with the term *verstehen*.[13] These critics received considerable sustenance from those who argued that the physical sciences themselves do not really proceed according to the rigid canons of the "scientific method." The so-called Kuhn-Feyerabend thesis, which suggests the noncumulative nature of scientific knowledge, was perhaps most influential in this regard.[14] Also insightful were the writings of Stephen Toulmin, who persuasively described the intuitive, imaginative processes of scientific discovery and concept formation.[15]

The main intellectual criticism of behavioralism, however, has been that the separation of facts and values—an essential tenet of the traditional scientific method—is unnatural and, in fact, impossible. The Kuhn-Feyerabend thesis was fruitfully combined with the sociological work of Karl Mannheim and others to demonstrate that all knowledge is socially-located and, hence, a function of particular purposes or interests. From this it could be persuasively argued that much behavioral research in fact emanates from, or is at least supportive of, certain implicit value positions.[16] The alleged separation of facts and values was thus shown to be a myth. Moreover, some critics argued further that the separation of facts and values, even if possible, would not be desirable. For the sterile and dispassionate collection of social facts would, by itself, amount to a betrayal of one's proper role as an active and committed member of the human community. Though these general lines of thought were by no means universally accepted, they were nonetheless among the reasons for the renewed interest in normative questions of urban politics.

A second source of this revitalization was largely historical or circumstantial in nature. I refer here to what may be called the discovery of the urban crisis. Of course, crucial in this regard were the incidents of collective violence that shook many American cities in the 1960s, most especially Detroit and Los Angeles. In a general sense, the riots served to revive the notion that our cities were in bad shape and that fundamental changes in social policy were called for. As expressions of discontent and frustration, they led to a new emphasis on severe social problems and prompted new approaches to these problems on the part of social scientists.

The impact of the urban crisis upon political scientists was, perhaps, special. Empiricists had found, in study after study, that American cities generally had pluralist political systems based on processes of negotiation and compromise among competing group interests.[17] Moreover, these observers had also concluded—for a variety of reasons—that such systems were in fact pretty good systems, providing relatively stable, responsive, and responsible methods for making important decisions. Pluralist democracy was alive and well in urban America, and nearly everyone thereby benefited. The riots shattered this presumption. They served to show that such an enthusiastic picture of the urban political process was, at best, incomplete. In particular, they seemed to show that a significant portion of the urban population was in fact being left out of the decision process and was not benefiting adequately from urban public policies.[18]

At least two consequences followed from this. First, many urbanists were forced to revise their empirical theories of community power.[19] The pluralist model, especially in its simpler forms, no longer seemed to fit the facts, if it ever did, and thus new models or revisions of the old ones were forthcoming. Second, and more important for our purposes, the urban crisis reawakened scholars to the importance of normative questions. By suggesting the inadequacies of existing structures, however characterized, the riots of the 1960s prompted many political scientists to shift their attention from mere explication to some level of evaluation and prescription. The focus became not merely what *is* the case but also, and perhaps more urgently, what *should be* the case. There was, in short, a growing and still vital preoccupation with improving, rather than merely explaining urban political systems.

The third reason for the rebirth of urban normative theory was a political outgrowth of the previous one. Specifically, the urban crisis of the 1960s had an impact not only on academic political scientists but on government as well.

The federal government in particular began to turn its attention increasingly to the problems of our cities. This attention manifested itself in the vast growth of federal grants-in-aid to cities, and in the formulation of more or less explicit (and more or less publicized) programs for dealing with urban problems. Such activity made normative speculation about urban politics a more salient endeavor. For political theorists could, at least conceivably, have a real impact upon public policy. The reputed influence of Michael Harrington's *The Other America*, and the elevation of such urbanists as Edward Banfield and Daniel Moynihan to positions of apparent access and influence, undoubtedly contributed to this feeling. Urban social science mattered, its impact could be felt, and the mere fact of increased governmental involvement sowed the seeds of controversy. The writings of a Banfield or Moynihan, though inherently inflammatory, became even more so by virtue of their semiofficial status.

And thus we have witnessed, in the past fifteen years, a series of vigorous controversies concerning the nature of urban problems and policies. Phrases like community control, benign neglect, maximum feasible participation, black power, open housing, and revenue sharing have been the symbols of controversy in the corridors of power, in the mass media, and in the academy as well. I do not mean to paint an excessively simple or one-sided picture of the current status of urban political science. American universities and research institutes are populated with an abundance of scholars who conduct research from a wide variety of empirical perspectives. The concern with understanding how cities operate is by no means dead. Indeed, it is certain that the vast majority of published studies on urban politics still have primarily explanatory concerns, and that is probably as it should be.

However, the normative mood, so subdued in earlier periods, has now moved to center stage. The most interesting current writing on urban politics is deeply normative in its approach, writing that attempts to identify key problems and, more importantly, attempts to tell us what we ought to do about those problems. Of course, it is *ideological* writing in particular that is of greatest interest to us and that commands our attention. But what is ideology and how does it differ from other kinds of political thought? It is to this more basic question that we now turn.

VARIETIES OF NORMATIVE POLITICAL THOUGHT

Any effort to evaluate and prescribe political institutions and actions in terms of moral or ethical criteria we shall call "normative." But normative political thought is not of a piece. A newspaper editorial recommending a change in local election laws is, in a very real sense, an example of normative political thought. It is primarily concerned with prescription and moral judgment, as opposed to mere description and empirical analysis. But then, so too is Plato's *Republic,* or Aristotle's *Politics,* or Hegel's *Philosophy of Right.* These latter, that is, share with the editorial a concern for what *ought* to be, rather than just what *is.* All must therefore be considered examples of normative political thought.

And yet, such cases are clearly so different from one another, not only in terms of intellectual worth but also in terms of style and content, that the simple phrase *normative political thought* would seem to be virtually meaningless without considerable qualification. We need some way of distinguishing and sorting out the intentions and structures of a wide variety of normative writings—a newspaper editorial, a Platonic dialogue, a judicial opinion, a party platform, a statement of personal faith, or a systematic and general treatise on political ethics. Scholars have in fact worked long at developing an adequate taxonomy of political thought, one that would not only distinguish the various kinds of normative writing from one another but, in addition, would further our understanding of political theory itself. Unfortunately, these efforts have met with mixed success at best.

One common strategy has been to distinguish "political philosophy" from "political ideology." There is, however, considerable disagreement as to how each of these terms should be employed. For example, in a widely read discussion, P. H. Partridge refers to political philosophy as that which attempts to connect conclusions about politics with some kind of wider (nonpolitical) philosophic system.[20] In other words, political philosophers have "tried to derive political and social conclusions from more general beliefs about the nature of reality."[21] The implication is that political philosophies are essentially *descriptions* of underlying political reality, of the essence of politics. On the other hand, Partridge identifies ideology as all political thought that emphasizes ethical reflection. That is, ideology is concerned with" elaborating and advocating conceptions of the good life."[22]

Now this seems to be a useful categorization. For there does seem to be a certain class of especially "philosophic" thinkers whose political ideas are explicitly linked to general principles of philosophy. Plato, St. Augustine, and Hegel would be obvious examples. Unfortunately, however, Partridge's is by no means the only useful or attractive taxonomy we have. Thus, in a more recent discussion, Nannerl O. Keohane also distinguishes political philosophy from ideology. But her conceptualization is a rather different one, depending mainly on the quality or profundity of discourse.[23] For Keohane, political philosophy seeks to "penetrate beneath or beyond appearances to a more basic reality, something more profound and lasting than that which can be immediately apprehended."[24] In so doing, political philosophy is characterized by "abstract, higher-order, comprehensive statements about life" which may have metaphysical *or* ethical concerns.[25] In contrast, ideology is characterized as merely a tool for the political partisan, "a shorthand guide to action," to be judged by its "utility for the performer in a certain situation, given his goals, his temperament, his opponents, his abilities, his allies."[26]

Clearly, "political philosophy" means one thing for Partridge, something quite different for Keohane. But indeed, the variations go far beyond this. For Leo Strauss, political *philosophy* is fundamentally moral inquiry about politics, whereas for John Plamenatz it is largely an analytic enterprise aimed at uncovering and solving problems of political language. On the other hand, Plamenatz describes political *theory* as "systematic thinking about the purposes of government," while Strauss uses this term when considering mere descriptions of the nature of politics.[27] The term "ideology" has experienced an even wider range of diverse uses. It is variously understood as a call to action, an explicit and closed system of thought, a demagogic "short-circuiting" device, a justification for extremism, or a defense of the status quo. Indeed, for some writers virtually all social and political thinking is "ideological" in the sense of being socially-located.[28]

All of this is, to be sure, very unsatisfying. Indeed, it may strike one as a rather silly spectacle, an endless game of semantics without real purpose or hope of resolution. Yet, some kind of classificatory scheme is absolutely necessary if our field of inquiry—normative political thought—is to make any sense. The efforts of Partridge, Keohane, and others in the analytic tradition have been, I would argue, extremely useful in uncovering some of the linguistic and conceptual puzzles surrounding such words and phrases as political philosophy, political theory, and ideology. If they have failed to *solve* such puzzles, this in no way suggests that their efforts have been wasted. Rather, and more simply, it suggests only that any classificatory scheme we adopt can at best be a stipulated one which makes rational sense, which takes into account linguistic problems, but which, nonetheless, can make no claim to being objectively true.

The typology to be used here borrows from those mentioned above, and identifies three types of normative political thought—*political philosophy, ideology,* and *policy advocacy*. Two criteria are used to differentiate these from one another. First, *the types of normative political thought will be distinguished in terms of the aims and intentions that govern their production.* That is, they are distinct largely in terms of the purposes for which they are written. Especially relevant here is the question of *time-frame*. Some political writings are produced with specific and proximate events in mind, others with whole eras in mind, and still others for all the ages. An author who writes for all the ages is engaged in a very different kind of activity from one who is concerned only with current controversies; as a result the nature of his theory will also be very different. Second, *the types of normative political thought will be distinguished in terms of the degree to which judgments are based on explicit and systematically developed principles.* Many political writers postulate certain basic principles as merely given, or else presuppose them tacitly, even unwittingly. Others, however, refuse to assume such principles but, rather, seek to defend them rationally and comprehensively, arguing from well-defined premises to well-articulated and soundly justified conclusions. Again, the result is a different kind of political discourse, the goal of which is to develop arguments of broad scope and unassailable coherence.

Given these two criteria, I shall use the term *political philosophy* to refer to that literature which seeks to develop *systematic* normative principles of relatively *enduring and universal* application. To be sure, the political philosopher may have particular circumstances in mind when developing his ideas. Indeed, he may well be strongly influenced or motivated by proximate events. However, he is a political philosopher—as here defined—insofar as the principles he develops and expounds are, as far as we can tell, intended to apply to an exceedingly broad, nearly universal range of political circumstances.

Hobbes would be a paradigm case. Specifically, Hobbes would be considered a "political philosopher" because he self-consciously developed a series of normative political principles—relating to ideas of political obligation and natural law—that he considered to be more or less applicable or true in all historical situations. He did this despite his obvious interest in the politics of his day. *Leviathan* was written in a time of severe political upheaval, and its relevance for that upheaval can hardly be denied.[29] Yet a treatise the first book of which is portentously titled "Of Man" and which offers, in a systematic and comprehensive manner, basic political principles stated in the most general of terms can hardly be considered a mere *livre de circonstance*. Indeed, it is impossible to read *Leviathan* without concluding that its arguments are, in some sense, intended to apply to situations that go far beyond the historical/cultural contexts in which they were produced. On this account, then, virtually all the major theorists of the Western political tradition would be considered political philosophers. The great authors—Plato, Aristotle, St. Augustine, St. Thomas, Bodin, Locke, Rousseau, and Hegel—all sought to develop explicit and systematic principles of virtually universal application.

Ideology, on the other hand, is characterized by normative principles of a more proximate, time-bound nature. The ideologue is willing to accept certain things on faith; he is likely to postulate important principles as simply self evident; and he is *mainly* concerned with a particular historical situation or period. He is thus a partisan, and the principles he relies on—though perhaps relatively systematic—are intended to apply only to that particular situation and no other. Ideologies therefore tend to be written by less famous authors. Though potentially quite broad in content, their actual focus is on immediate states of affairs. Thus, for example, contemporary conservatives and liberals—authors such as Robert Nisbet or Robert Dahl—do have rather general and consistent theories, but their views are aimed at, and are really only applied to, relatively contemporary circumstances. As such, ideologies tend to be either critiques or defenses of existing political systems and practices; they do not explicitly develop or defend universally valid principles of government and politics. And to the extent that they make universal claims, they often do so only as *dicta*, that is, in an unsystematic or gratuitous fashion—for example, general assertions about equal rights or human dignity. A typical and familiar body of ideological thought, as here defined, would be the pamphlet literature of the American revolutionary period.

Finally, *policy advocacy* will refer to nongeneral normative writing, based on comparatively narrow, unsystematic principles. Like the ideologue, the policy advocate's purview is relatively time-bound. His judgments are by no means applicable to all settings. However, unlike the ideologue, the policy advocate does not invoke general and comprehensive systems of thought. Rather, he tends to be concerned in a practical or instrumental way only with a handful of specific policy areas.

Again, these distinctions are not to be regarded as fixed or absolute; they are intended as heuristic classificatory devices which I judge to be useful in ordering the sphere of normative political discourse and to which I have appended convenient, hopefully suggestive names. Even so, the dividing line between the three types is by no means exact. Thus, for example, Marx might be considered an ideologue, insofar as his prime concern was to criticize capitalist society in the nineteenth century. On the other hand, he was a political philosopher insofar as he systematically developed principles that were intended to be universally applicable, for example, the dialectical interpretation of history. Of course, there is much controversy as to the real nature of Marx's political thought. However, for our purpose the key variable is his intention. That is, at what level of generality was he attempting to operate, as far as we can tell? If his intention was to discover and elucidate universal principles, then by our standards he was a political philosopher, though not for that reason a good one. If, on the other hand, his efforts were involved less with the defense or application of universal principles than with the broad controversies of his day, then perhaps we would call him an ideologue (while seeking, of course, to purge that word of all pejorative implications).

The issue of precisely demarcating philosophy and ideology is further complicated by the fact that virtually all genuine political philosophers have also had ideological concerns.[30] Plato has been accused of being essentially a partisan and of writing political tracts aimed at influencing the controversies of his time. The writings of Machiavelli and Locke clearly had partisan implications. Even Hegel, perhaps the most self-consciously philosophic and universal of all political theorists, is frequently associated with the disputes of his day. The sorting out of philosophic and ideological intentions is, therefore, an extremely difficult task.

But there is an even more important sense in which ideologies and political philosophies are linked. For ideologies, though primarily concerned with proximate events, are typically based upon implicit and unspecified philosophic principles which shape the entire ideological enterprise. That is, while the intention of the ideologue is, by our definition, ideological, his point of view may nonetheless be entirely founded upon certain unstated principles of potentially universal application. In such a case, he is still an ideologue, for he has not systematically derived and justified those principles and, hence, his purpose is not to propagate them. On the other hand, there remains an essential philosophic core insofar as he is accepting and affirming, however passively and unconsciously, those same general premises. Thus, the ideology is somewhat more than merely an instrument of circumstance. It is, at least in part, a product of, and also a *purveyor* of, certain underlying principles of political philosophy; as a result, it can only be truly understood if those implicit and unstated foundations are revealed and understood.

It is at this interstice, somewhere within the gray area between political philosophy and ideology, that we can come closest to specifying the subject matter of the present book. Most normative approaches to contemporary urban politics are written by policy advocates, focusing on particular substantive problems and proposing particular practical solutions. Such writings, though obviously important, are not our concern here. At the other extreme, in the realm of what we would call genuine "urban political philosophy," we find, I would submit, very little. Which is simply to say that there are today few true political philosophers of city politics. There are no grand systems of urban political thought, no comprehensive treatises on urban political principles. However, in the middle ground, where ideology is infused with and founded upon, and at the same time faithfully serves and promotes, certain underlying principles of political philosophy—here is where one finds the significant normative theorizing about urban politics today. The writers I shall focus on are certainly not systematic political philosophers; but neither are they mere policy advocates. They are, rather, ideologues whose work is based upon and supportive of implicit philosophic principles.

ELEMENTS OF POLITICAL PHILOSOPHY

Clearly then, we have to know something about political philosophy in order to intelligently treat ideologies of the urban crisis. Political philosophers and their interpreters as well are involved in a distinctive intellectual enterprise—a discipline, if you will—with standards of judgment and modes of inquiry all its own. Like all disciplines, political philosophy is distinguished both by the questions it asks and, perhaps less clearly, by the methods it employs. But even more importantly, it is distinguished by its conceptual apparatus. That is, political philosophy is based upon a unique set of concepts which order its intellectual world and establish its disciplinary parameters. An elucidation of at least some of these concepts can thus help us understand the nature of the philosophic enterprise and, in so doing, help establish a framework for the analysis of urban political ideologies.

Of course, the conceptual apparatus of political philosophy is complex and quite extensive. It includes concepts that pertain to formal institutional relationships, for example, democracy or representation or citizenship. It also includes purely ethical notions, especially notions of justice and desert. It involves concepts that pertain to individuals (e.g., liberty or rights), to groups of individuals (faction or class or community), and to relations between individuals or groups (equality or contract). Such conceptions constitute a universe of discourse which unites those writers of the past and present who have created the landmark works of the tradition, from the dialogues of Plato to the contemporary essays of Arendt, Oakeshott, and Rawls, among others.

The complexity and breadth of this set of concepts makes a quick precis of the field difficult, indeed impossible.[31] There are, nonetheless, certain foundational notions which are perhaps prior, which define the tradition more clearly than any others, and which, when analyzed in any particular case, are especially revealing of the essence of a theorist's work. Four such notions—we can call them themes or conceptual fields—will be outlined here, notions of *political obligation,* the *public realm, practical reason,* and the *nature of political man*. It is my view that any systematic treatise of political philosophy necessarily deals, directly or indirectly, with all four of these themes; and, further, that the approach to them is, in large part, what distinguishes one treatise from another. That is, if we understand a particular political philosopher's approach to these four themes, then we have understood to a significant degree the intellectual core of his political thought as a whole.

The problem of *political obligation* is central to all political philosophy. Specifically, it raises the following normative question: Under what circumstances is one morally obligated to obey the law? As such, it assumes a basic, underlying tension between the interests, desires, and needs of the individual on one hand and those of society on the other hand. In brief, society is not truly society unless it is characterized by a certain degree of peace and harmony, functional coordination, and conformity. Politically, this means among other things that its laws must be obeyed. The individual's will must, in effect, bend to the will of society. But the individual, on the other hand, demands an opportunity to be free, distinctive, and nonconforming. Indeed, laws are typically designed to prevent the individual from doing what he would otherwise want or need to do. Thus, for political society to exist in any kind of meaningful and legitimate way, it must include a theory—i.e., a set of reasons—as to why the individual *should* submit and why society can legitimately *coerce* or punish those who refuse to do so.32

For some critics, the problem of political obligation is essentially a modern problem, the more or less exclusive concern of Thomas Hobbes and his successors in the Western liberal tradition.33 For others, it is rather a characteristic theme of medieval political thought, especially in its effort to reconcile secular and ecclesiastical authority.34 In my judgment, however, the problem is treated, explicitly or implicitly, by virtually all serious and systematic writers on politics. Its roots can be found in the classical period, for example, in such foundation statements of our literary heritage as Sophocles's *Antigone* and the *Apology* of Socrates; and its development can be traced in the history of political philosophy itself, from Book 2 of Plato's *Republic* onward.

Indeed, the centrality of the problem of political obligation can hardly be overestimated. To be sure, there is little agreement among the great theorists concerning the true basis of obligation. For some, one should obey because of the philosophically discoverable dictates of natural law. For others, obedience is rooted in the will of God, as revealed to us, for example, in Scripture. And for still others, obligation is essentially a question of self-interest and the rational calculation of expected utilities. Indeed, there are numerous other approaches. But in all cases, a theory of political obligation is essentially a response to this most basic of all political questions: How is legitimate political society possible?

To have provided a systematic and coherent answer to such a question is to have achieved quite a bit. However, there is another question which is of equal importance to political philosophy: What is the nature of the *public realm?* By "public realm" I refer to that area of activity which is appropriate for legitimately constituted public authorities. In effect, it defines the range of issues or concerns which governmental and other political entities are entitled to consider. Thus, if the first question asks how government can be legitimate, the second question asks what governments ought to do. That is, we are concerned now with the purpose, rather than the justification, of political authority.[35]

Of course, for it to make sense the notion of the "public realm" must imply the existence of a "private realm," an area of activity in which government should not be involved. And thus, the problem of demarcating the private and the public realm has become, like the problem of political obligation, basic to political philosophy, and has preoccupied virtually all systematic writers on politics. Again, various solutions have been offered. For some, the range of legitimate political activity is wide indeed, comprising nearly all facets of what we today would call social life. For others, the proper public realm is severely circumscribed, limited to only certain special areas that affect especially large numbers of individuals in specific ways. And for still others, political authorities can legitimately define their own areas of endeavor as they please, provided that they are themselves duly and appropriately authorized. But in each case, the nature of the public realm determines, in effect, the purposes of political life. Thus, for example, in the *kallipolis* of Plato's *Republic* the purpose of politics is largely educative, to train individuals to perform those functions best suited to their natures and necessary for the health of society; and the activities of the public realm are structured accordingly. For Aristotle, on the other hand, politics essentially provides a context in which men of ability can attain a peculiarly political or civic kind of excellence; it is an arena in which men can rule and be ruled in turn. For certain liberals, government functions merely to enforce law and order, to prevent people from doing harm to one another, largely by threatening to punish transgressors; whereas for certain medieval writers, government's central function is moral, to create a context favorable to the practice of Christianity. In all such cases, the effort is to differentiate political activity from all nonpolitical forms of endeavor, and to define the former's necessary and characteristic attributes.

These two themes or conceptual fields—political obligation and the public realm—comprise what we may call the basic principles of political philosophy. They are foundational notions which spawn various other derivative concepts such as authority and sovereignty, power and liberty, representation and consent, and the like. Thus, in considering the work of any major political philosopher, the initial task is to uncover, specify, and evaluate the author's particular theory of political obligation and of the public realm. This task is rarely easy. In many cases, for example, a theory of obligation must be pieced together in various ways and from various sources. To my knowledge, Plato in his mature work explicitly considers the question of political obligation only rarely; yet, that his writing contains, at least implicitly, a theory of obligation is in my view beyond dispute.[36] In other cases, the precise meaning of an author's theory may well be unclear. Perhaps no major political philosopher offered as explicit and systematic a theory of obligation as Hobbes; yet the critical debate among Hobbes scholars concerning the true meaning of that theory is, to say the least, intense.[37] Thus, the task is a difficult one. Nonetheless, it is essential. For a work of political philosophy simply cannot be comprehended unless its basic political principles, those concerning obligation and the public realm, are uncovered and explicated.

Such notions, however, do not ordinarily arise out of thin air, nor are they simply self-justifying. Rather, they are themselves dependent, at least in part, on certain prior intellectual positions. In particular, it must be recalled that principles of political obligation and of the public realm are normative principles. As such, they involve assertions of good and bad, or of right and wrong, in the moral sense of those words. Hence, for an author to make judgments regarding, say, political obligation, it is necessary that he have some idea as to how moral judgments are made in the first place. To put it more simply, every political philosophy rests upon an explicit ethical theory of some kind, a theory of *practical reason.*

Following Kant, if we define "theoretical reason" as the mode of thought concerned with what *is*, then practical reason is the mode of thought concerned with what one *ought* to do. As should be amply clear, the process by which acceptable practical judgments can be made is a matter of considerable dispute. For example, there are those who would have us rely on the so-called faculty of natural reason, and those who would invoke, instead, divine revelation and faith. A contemporary theorist like John Rawls would require that we decide beneath a "veil of ignorance," while Nietzsche, on the other hand, would despair of making any reliable moral judgments at all. The point here is not to offer an outline of various ethical views but, rather, to suggest that all political philosophers must have some notion as to how assertions of right and wrong can be justified. Without such a notion, theories of political obligation and of the public realm would be like objects in a surrealist painting, hanging suspended in midair without any visible support.

Notions of practical reason are themselves, however, based on certain still prior intellectual positions. While these may be various and complex, I would argue that virtually all ethical theories, hence all political philosophies, rely on at least some premises regarding the essential *nature of man* and the nature of man's place in the world. For example, the Christian view that valid ethical judgments must be based on divine revelation is nonsensical unless one assumes that human beings are creations of a God and are, in some way, capable of receiving His message. Similarly, the notion that right and wrong can be gleaned through natural reason necessarily assumes that the faculty of natural reason is a part of human nature. Indeed, ethical theories are, as often as not, straightforward deductions from certain views regarding the nature of man, views which generally have the status of unproved, perhaps unprovable, but presumably plausible premises.

In sum, I am suggesting that the structure of any systematic political philosophy is essentially threefold, involving (1) underlying premises regarding the nature of man, (2) a theory of practical reason and ethical judgment, and (3) specific approaches to the problems of political obligation and the public realm. Moreover, as should be implicit in much of the foregoing, this structure can be fruitfully looked at as a structure in the true sense, one in which the three kinds of elements have specifiable, identifiable relations. The following schema is illustrative:

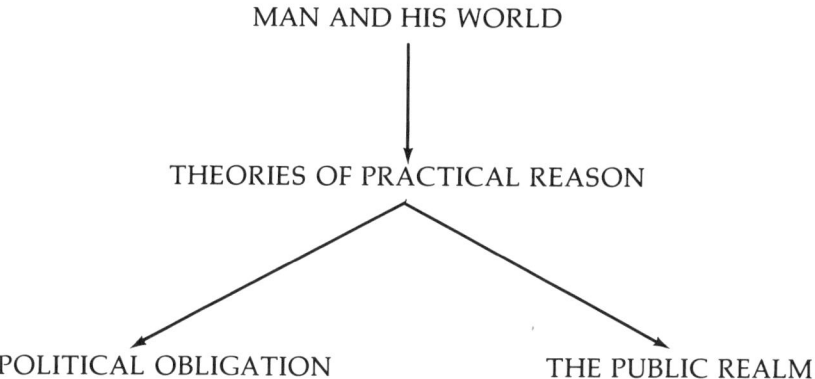

Thus, for any political philosophy, a theory of practical reason should be discernible, but one which is also a deduction from certain premises regarding human nature. Similarly, basic political principles regarding obligation and the public realm should be discoverable, but again principles which are dependent on the theory of practical reason. To truly approach a work of political philosophy, then, the critical task is not merely to specify the three levels of analysis but also to identify and evaluate the nature of the *linkages* between the three. This involves asking, for example, to what extent Hobbes's theory of political obligation truly follows from his general moral theory; or to what extent Kant's premises regarding man necessarily entail a particular moral stance. Such questions are concerned with the cogency of argument, with rational or logical consistency, with the coherence and soundness of a particular bit of reasoning.

This, then, provides a critical protocol for dealing with treatises in political philosophy: first, to specify an author's approach to the three levels of conceptualization and, second, to evaluate the adequacy of the linkages between those levels. Can this protocol, however, be applied to those works which are *ideological* in nature, which fail, that is, to offer comprehensive and systematic rationales for the principles they invoke or, indeed, which invoke those principles only tacitly? My judgment is that it can, with modifications. For insofar as ideological systems are repositories of philosophic material, such material can itself be dredged up and examined for coherence and plausibility. Indeed, if there is in fact a philosophic core within each ideology, then that core can—and must—be uncovered and subjected to critical scrutiny.

As indicated above, ideologies tend to reflect deep-seated and philosophic principles, including and especially principles of the kind discussed in this section. Of course, given his purposes we cannot expect the ideologue to explicate and develop such principles in any satisfying manner, even if he were fully aware of them. And yet, they are there, tacit but pivotal, orienting the ideology, giving it a direction and a pedigree—an intellectual heritage which permits us to place it more clearly within the history of ideas and which gives it some shape and substance. We can therefore examine the ideologies of urban politics with a view toward uncovering, explicating, and evaluating the implicit premises upon which they rest. Since each ideology is based upon unarticulated but nevertheless essential principles of political philosophy, our job is to unearth those principles, to demonstrate in just what ways the ideology is dependent upon them, and to show what about them is convincing and what is not. Only by penetrating to the philosophic core can we make ideologies of urban politics come alive as ideologies; and indeed, only in this way can we truly appreciate and assess their meaning and their value.

The Ideologies of Urban Politics

It has already been suggested that there is a burgeoning normative literature on urban politics. This literature includes a wide variety of approaches which are not easily summarized or categorized. Indeed, they can only be understood and effectively ordered if their philosophic foundations are exposed and examined. A complete inventory of such writing is not possible or desirable here. However, some brief suggestions can be useful in introducing the subject and indicating its scope.

To begin with, then, we have a series of writings often associated with various notions of "municipal reform." Some of these deal with the institutional structure of urban government, advocating systematic reforms, such as council-manager government, aimed at eliminating the evils of machine politics. Others emphasize the importance of personnel systems or electoral systems and seek to combat the unsavory politics of patronage. A third group takes a more issue-oriented approach to reform, focusing on problems of poverty and social welfare and proposing a variety of substantive (rather than structural) innovations. A fourth group, related to all of the previous, is concerned with the notion of rational planning and with the associated goals of efficiency and economy.

In addition to the literature on reform, we also have writings which emphasize the political importance of the urban neighborhood. Again, a variety of approaches can be included here. Some of these focus on the idea of neighborhood government or community control, arguing that the neighborhood unit ought to be the primary locus of legitimate governmental authority in the city. Others argue for political decentralization in which the administration of citywide policy is undertaken at the community level. A related view emphasizes the political sociology of American cities and stresses the need to overcome the alleged atomization, alienation, and fragmentation of urban social relations. Still others focus on the need for militant political activism, usually arising out of the community context and typically aimed at redressing various racial or economic grievances.

We must also point to a variety of self-consciously conservative approaches to urban politics. In accord with general conservative notions, these writings often caution against precipitous changes in urban public policy, arguing that familiar practices, though perhaps imperfect, may well be superior to new alternatives whose impact cannot be accurately predicted. The conservative viewpoint typically regards political man as by nature deeply flawed and, consequently, incapable of much self-conscious improvement. As a result, urbanists of this persuasion tend to view city politics as something of a holding process the main purpose of which is to manage conflict and effect only minor political adjustments where feasible.

Other writers view urban politics in perhaps more global terms. For example, some regard the city as a system of class struggle and argue for a radical redistribution of power and material benefits. Others see urban government as a marketplace in which public goods are produced and consumed according to the laws of supply and demand. Still others view American cities in terms of classical notions of politics, emphasizing the need for public spaces, for civic virtue and active citizenship; while another approach concerns itself with the proper place of cities in the federal system, often arguing for greater local independence from state and federal authorities.

This partial listing illustrates the considerable variety of contemporary normative approaches to urban politics. As should now be amply apparent, a main theme of this book is that summarizing and analyzing these diverse approaches can be most effectively accomplished by unearthing their philosophic foundations and by discovering the implicit intellectual presuppositions that mold and direct each of them. Most classifications of urban political theory fail to do so. They typically focus on the superficial characteristics of various theories, or rely on simplistic, seemingly self-evident distinctions. For instance, some authors distinguish, as I have above, "reform" theories from theories of "community control." Such a classification, however, is problematic and ultimately unsatisfying. The word *reform*, for example, is a protean term. Though generally associated with progressivism and the efficiency and economy movement, one can find many other quite different connotations. In New York City, "reform Democrat" is a term applied to liberals; for Robert Bish and Vincent Ostrom, reform means a return to a market model of urban politics; indeed, the Age of Reform itself was supported in certain respects by many distinctly "unreformed" politicians. In its most general political sense, reform connotes a more or less rational and controlled (i.e., nonrevolutionary) attempt to ameliorate the process and product of government. But of course this is precisely what many advocates of decentralization and community control have had in mind, i.e., a nonrevolutionary but significant restructuring of urban governments. In general, then such conventional taxonomies fail to provide satisfactory distinctions.

A philosophic approach is, I think, preferable. It allows us to explore the unstated premises of a particular theory, thereby disclosing its real thrust and importance. The meanings of specific arguments, the sources of key propositions, the logic of an author's approach, and the relationship of a theory to other theories—these are what distinguish one set of ideas from another, and what provide each with substance and focus.

The chapters that follow focus on three ideologies of the urban crisis—managerialism, communalism, and possessive-individualism. My purpose will be to outline the basic tenets of each, to identify their various impacts on American urban politics, and to discover their underlying and implicit philosophic foundations. Each ideology will be treated in what we might call its "ideal character," i.e., as an abstraction from reality, an ideal type, a composite that summarizes and defines a range of related approaches to urban politics.[38] Just as there is no single thing in the real world that is ideal socialism or communism or liberalism, so too there are many kinds of managerialists, many kinds of communalists, many kinds of possessive-individualists. Each of our ideologies, therefore, is in effect a general *orientation* toward the urban crisis, a perspective or perhaps even a mood which is shared to a greater or lesser degree by a host of various writers. What unites such writers, what brings them together under a single ideological rubric, is the fact that their work springs from the same philosophic soil. Managerialists, for example, may disagree with one another on any number of issues. But insofar as they share certain implicit views of the nature of politics, of morality, and of mankind itself, they stand together as representatives of a single intellectual tradition.

Our three ideologies of urban politics are thus vehicles of a deeper, more venerable opposition than would at first seem to be the case. The differences between managerialists, communalists, and possessive-individualists are in fact manifestations of tensions that spring from deep within Western thought and that have defined the political landscape since the beginnings of the modern age. Ultimately, then, it is in these terms that we have to understand the urban crisis.

2. THE MANAGERIAL MOOD

The idea of "municipal reform" has had a major impact on American urban politics throughout this century. As an example, one can point to the rather remarkable history of the council-manager form of city government. Devised around the turn of the century, its precise origins unclear, the council-manager plan quickly became one of the great symbols of the urban reform movement.[1] Adopted by Richard S. Childs and the National Municipal League, the plan came to stand for all the best in "good government": professional administration, nonpartisanship, the short ballot, centralization of authority. As such, it came to be seen as a major weapon in the fight against the venality, the wasteful and immoral particularism of machine politics. Virtually every systematic treatment of the progressive era notes the importance of the municipal reform movement and its role in the propagation of reform ideals.[2]

What is perhaps most astonishing about the history of the council-manager plan, however, is its rather sudden popularity. Council-manager government, or something rather like it, was adopted for the first time in 1908 by the community of Staunton, Virginia, a small city in the central section of the state, not generally known as a pacesetter in the world of municipal politics. Yet, only twelve years later, in 1920, this previously unknown structure of government, an entirely new and untested mechanism, had been implemented in as many as 158 American municipalities. Its rise since then has been perhaps even more spectacular. By 1970, well over two thousand American cities had adopted the plan; over fifty percent of all municipalities between ten thousand and five hundred thousand population utilized some kind of council-manager government.[3]

Of course, there are many reasons why a particular city might adopt the manager plan. An especially bad experience with the party system, the presence of an aggressive and power-hungry city council, the availability of professional/ managerial talent—such factors could and did prompt particular localities to hop aboard the bandwagon. But the remarkable popularity of council-manager government must nonetheless be regarded as, in large part, a testament to the appeal of reformist ideas qua ideas.

In a similar vein, one can point to a variety of institutions, concepts, and procedures associated with the practice of "urban planning." Though people have always laid plans, the notion of planning as a specific method of collective action and as a conscious technique of government is of fairly recent origin. More specifically, we can argue with some assurance that "urban planning," other than merely physical planning, was virtually unknown as an ongoing function in nineteenth-century America, where the activity of governing was understood to involve a series of more or less effective responses to particular problems, an instinctive, pragmatic process ordered only—and perhaps only sporadically—by the rules of law.[4] The idea of a rationally planned polity—which, as we shall see, is perhaps most clearly traceable to certain intellectual currents of the eighteenth century—lay nascent in America until the rise of progressivism. In the search for a "public interest," and for a *method* by which the evils of private power could be eliminated, an answer was found in planning, i.e., the idea of a public policy devised rationally by trained experts and implemented with an overriding regard for matters of efficiency and economy.[5]

While this notion has perhaps been most widely applied to matters of land use and housing, it in fact describes an important method of looking at virtually all of the problems of urban government.[6] Its influence has been undeniable. The first official city planning commission seems to have been established in 1907 in Hartford, one year before the council-manager plan got its start. The rise of planning since that time, as an integral and ongoing part of American city government, has been spectacular. Adrian and Press report that by 1960 over ninety percent of all American cities of at least ten thousand population had official planning agencies or commissions.⁷

Many other examples could be enlisted to demonstrate the influence of reformist ideas. The augmentation in the size and scope of urban bureaucracies, the increase in federal expenditures to state and local governments, the multiplicity of rationally devised programs which increasingly order and constrain the activities of local entities, the professionalization and consequent "depoliticization" of the agents of city government—all of these point to the efficacy of ideas and methods associated with the so-called reformist impulse in American politics.

As indicated in the previous chapter, the word reform is a dangerous one, filled with a variety of obscuring connotations and applicable to a wide range of political forms and ideas. Thus far, I have been using it in a rather conventional sense. However, for the sake of precision the perspective here considered requires a somewhat clearer terminology. As the following discussion will show, the line of thought we are concerned with, and which we shall treat in its ideal character, understands government as essentially an *enterprise* aimed at solving social problems and structured in such a manner that the *management* of the enterprise can be effectively and fruitfully undertaken.⁸ This is, in short, *a managerial perspective*. It describes a relatively coherent approach to the problems of the political world, and also a distinctive and important *style* of political activity. As such, it is a unique intellectual perspective, one which is based upon, and which serves to propagate, certain important and controversial philosophic principles.

THE MANAGERIAL POSITION

The central features of the managerial perspective may be formulated as follows:

1. *A propensity to operate explicitly and pointedly in terms of a conception of the "public interest."* Of course, all political ideologies and philosophies purport to have some such notion of the public interest, the common good, the interest of the community, and the like. The managerial perspective, however, postulates a public interest that is separate from and beyond

any kind of particular interest. The implications of this are complex and will be explored below. But what it most clearly entails is the view that particular, private interests—i.e., "special interests"—are a threat to the good health of society.

2. *An image of government as an apparatus for solving problems.* The proper function of government can be understood in a variety of ways. The managerial perspective tends to under-emphasize the deliberative, educative, communicative, and moral functions. Rather, it sees government as essentially a mechanism, a tool which can be used to obtain certain socially desired results. Many traditions see good government as an end in itself; the managerial ideology regards government as merely a means to some other end.

3. *An emphasis on expertise and professionalism in performing public duties.* Government requires a certain special competence, and this requirement itself becomes a fundamental tenet of the managerial perspective. Managerialism is thus an elitist ideology; it is based on the notion that some members of society are, by training or temperament, more capable than others of guiding the governmental apparatus. There is also the implication that the governmental function is largely a technical one, a matter of effectively *managing* the public enterprise. The capable few are thus superior in a technical rather than a moral sense. The citizenry should play a more or less secondary role, functioning largely as a source of social values.

4. *A rejection of "politics," understood as a process of conflict and negotiation among particular interests.* In many ways, this feature is a summary of the first three. The emphasis on problem solving in the public interest, as determined by experts, demands that the governmental process be above and beyond the mean world of politics. Conflict, compromise, parochialism, corruption—these are symptoms of power in the wrong hands, the great evils of political society. The managerial tradition seeks to overcome these evils, to restore responsibility and competence, to give power once and for all to those members of society most able to exercise it.

We might wish to trace these views to thinkers and movements of our earliest history. One might see elements of them, for example, in the Colonial concept of "stewardship," perhaps best symbolized by the figure of John Cotton. Stewardship prescribed a system of government relying upon "active, capable men, excellent administrators rather than speculative thinkers, stewards of the public interest."[9] This would be, of course, an elitist system, run for the good of everyone by those few who had the most ability. It demanded strong leadership for the purpose of producing a well-managed, well-ordered society. But it was not quite managerialism. For it is by no means clear that Massachusetts Bay, for example, was primarily a problem-solving entity. Its goal was to establish a harmonious, well-knit social order, a community, rather than simply a mechanism for securing the welfare of each and all. Moreover, the Calvinist roots of Colonial society tended to emphasize the moral and theological purposes of the political community, and to establish not technocracy (if such a thing would have even been possible in the seventeenth century) but theocracy; the class of stewards was not merely more competent but also closer to God.[10] Thus, if Puritan political theory foreshadows the managerial temper, it does so only in a general, unfocused way.

One might also look to the Constitutional period for forerunners of the managerial perspective. Especially relevant would be such Federalist thinkers as Hamilton and Adams, and their views regarding the indolence and selfishness of the common man, the existence of a "natural aristocracy," and the desirability of energetic government. Again, however, the correspondence with the managerial temper is rather vague. For just as the Colonial polity cannot be adequately understood as a problem-solving enterprise association, so the Federalist ideal is best regarded more as a legal or constitutional entity, designed to protect liberty and property rather than to solve specific social problems.

In fact, the managerial perspective in America can probably be best traced to a much more proximate era. Indeed, this is at least in part a result of the fact that the philosophic bases of managerialism were not really formulated until the eighteenth century and not adequately elaborated and disseminated until quite a bit later. In any case, the managerial perspective as related to urban politics has its sources in a variety of nineteenth- and twentieth-century American political and intellectual movements including progressivism, scientific management, municipal reform and—somewhat less clearly—democratic socialism, the single tax movement, the Square Deal, the New Freedom, the New Deal, and so on. All of these movements tended to embrace, in one form or another, a managerial perspective. They featured an approach to government emphasizing problem solving, expertise, administration, and the public interest. As such, they had an enormous influence on American political history, some aspects of which are especially worth mentioning here.

First, it is widely noted that the managerial mood was in some way connected with middle-class values and ideas. Perhaps the clearest and most influential exposition of this theme is Hofstadter's, who wrote as follows:

> Populism had been overwhelmingly rural and provincial. The ferment of the Progressive era was urban, middle class, and nationwide. Above all, Progressivism differed from Populism in the fact that the middle classes of the cities not only joined the trend toward protest but took over its leadership.[11]

In the early stages of the age of reform, according to Hofstadter, it was the "mugwump" type who came to symbolize the best in government. The ideal political man was "a well-to-do, well-educated, high-minded citizen, rich enough to be free from motives of . . . 'crass materialism,' [who] would be just the sort to put the national interest, as well as the interests of civic improvement, above personal motives or political opportunism."[12] Under the influence of professionals and the newly wealthy, however, the ideal soon became less aristocratic. Neutrality and public-spiritedness became associated less with wealth and cultivation than with training, education, and professionalism. As a result, "the Mugwump type was refashioned into the Progressive by the needs and demands of its own followers."[13] Perhaps more than anything else, the faith in science—in expertise—created this new image of the ideal political man as one who, by training and temperament, would be able to guide the machinery of government in an effective, productive, and businesslike manner, without reference to personal desires or private ambitions.

Perhaps the most important contemporary statement of this general orientation is to be found in Banfield and Wilson's work on political ethos.[14] According to their theory, citizens tend to be of two types, either "public regarding" or "private regarding." Public-regarding citizens disavow self-interest narrowly understood, and tend to act in terms of the good of the political system as a whole. According to Banfield and Wilson's research, such people are usually middle-class or upper-class, and are not likely to have strong ethnic identities. Private-regarding people, on the other hand, place narrow self-interest over other considerations. They tend to vote in order to maximize their immediate material advantage. Lower-class and working-class ethnics are, according to Banfield and Wilson, most likely to be private regarding. It should be noted that the evidence for these propositions has been vigorously and justly criticized.[15] Indeed, there is still no certain knowledge as to who is likely to be public regarding and who is not, or even whether these terms are appropriate for explaining political behavior. But what is important for our purposes is the fact that the progressive ideal still survives, and influences those who study urban politics. The well-known finding, for example, that the council-manager form of government has most often been adopted by largely white, middle-class suburbs (particularly in the West) has typically been explained in terms of the ethos theory.[16]

It is equally important in historical terms to note that municipal reform has manifested itself in a variety of ways. Of course, I shall be contending that the ideas presented in this chapter constitute a single and coherent way of looking at the political world. However, in historical and practical terms, the impact of the managerial perspective has been complex. More specifically, we can point to at least three different kinds of managerial innovation, each of which has been enormously important in shaping contemporary urban politics in the United States. These three may be termed structural, procedural, and substantive.

Structural innovation involves the designation and ordering of governmental institutions. The concern of the managerial perspective is to structure government in such a way that objective expertise can be most effectively utilized. Toward this end, as indicated above, much emphasis was placed on the council-manager form, a system of government designed to centralize administrative authority in the hands of a single professional (the city manager) who is responsible to the city council and, presumably, to his profession. By relying on a well-trained and typically "cosmopolitan" individual, the dual goals of efficiency and neutrality could be achieved. The degree to which council-manager government has lived up to these expectations will be considered shortly.[17] But its supporters have been enthusiastic and, as history shows, extremely persuasive.

Other structural or systemic innovations have been instituted for similar reasons. An alternative to the council-manager plan is the "commission plan," which has fallen out of favor in the last decade but is still used in a few large cities including Portland, Oregon. (Indeed, as of 1980, about four percent of all American cities with a population of five thousand or more were governed by the commission form in some variety.) The institution of the nonpartisan ballot, designed to eliminate the corrupting consequences of party politics, has been adopted in countless American cities during this century. Similarly, the at-large system of councilmanic districting has been a popular reform replacing the ward system which was thought to foster particularism and machine politics. Equally popular has been the independent board or commission, intended to ensure an "apolitical" approach to certain technical or cultural problems of public concern.

The most recent example of structural innovation has been the effort to promote metropolitanwide government in the United States. Metro-reform is, in many ways, characteristic of managerialism in general, with its emphasis on centralization, efficiency, and antiparticularism. While metrogovernment of one kind or another has been adopted in a few areas (most notably Jacksonville, Indianapolis, and Nashville), it has in general been very unpopular. This has largely been because suburban areas have sought to maintain their social and political autonomy; it cannot be said to indicate any significant attenuation in the popularity of the managerial mood.

Structural innovations have in many cases been accompanied by *procedural* ones. The latter refer essentially to the actual conduct of the governmental process and, again, are aimed at efficiency and competence. Of course, the structural proposals outlined above do, in themselves, tend to influence the processes of government. However, more specific procedural innovations have had at least an equal impact. Historically most important in this regard was the establishment of civil service or, more generally, the merit system. Beginning in 1883 with the creation of the federal civil service, this kind of personnel system has become typical in American urban government. The merit sytem, of course, includes a wide variety of specific devices. Independent civil service commissions are established to ensure that personnel decisions are based on proper criteria. Qualifying examinations are frequently employed as standards for determining merit. Explicit rules concerning tenure and dismissal are instituted so as to ensure a professional, nonpolitical government. Such devices are designed to reform the day-to-day processes of government so that venal political influence can be kept to a minimum. Professionals, whose positions are based on merit rather than patronage, are, according to the theory, insulated from unsavory pressures and are able to effectively pursue the public interest.

Of course, such devices by no means ensure true procedural change. There are numerous ways of avoiding or circumventing civil service regulations, and nearly all city governments do so, at least to some extent. Nonetheless, it is the theory that we are interested in. And it is fair to say that those forces responsible for implementing and maintaining merit systems have in mind the same general notions as those supporting structural innovation.

The merit system has been related to, and often is coincident with, the increasingly bureaucratization of urban government. There have been significant bureaucratizing trends throughout this century, generally involving increased reliance on administrative authority. The rational procedures described by Max Weber are not always, or even usually, followed.[18] But the intellectual impetus behind bureaucratization is nonetheless informed by an often fervent belief in the efficacy of rational, hierarchical processes.

The third type of managerial innovation is *substantive* in nature. Here I refer to the tendency on the part of city governments to broaden their scope of activities, to undertake ambitious policy initiatives designed to improve the general quality of urban life. Indeed, we are in a period where urban politicians speak not so much of laws or decisions but, rather, of "programs" and "plans." Perhaps the operative phrase here is "social engineering."[19] Increasingly, urban governments have attempted to rationally plan the lives of their citizens, to engineer or orchestrate social, economic, and political relations on the basis of administratively generated analyses.

Originally, city planning was concerned largely with matters of land use, housing, and transportation. A planner was one who viewed the city as essentially an ecological entity.[20] His goal was to attain the most efficient and functional mix of spatial uses. To achieve this, growth would have to be channeled, roads and rail systems optimally located, residential development intelligently managed, and the like. But today, planners define their roles rather more broadly. As Andreas Faludi notes, the direction of planning

> is away from a concern purely with the *physical* enviroment and towards intentionally rational, comprehensive planning; away from a primarily practice-oriented profession towards greater reliance on theoretical understanding; and away from the domination of planning by architects and engineers towards opening of its ranks to various disciplines, notably in the social sciences.[21]

Melvin Webber adds that

> the simple one-to-one cause-and-effect links that once tied houses and neighborhoods to behavior and welfare are coming to be seen as but strands in highly complex webs that, in turn, are woven by the intricate and subtle relations that mark social, psychic, economic, and political systems.[22]

Webber's conclusion is that "planning for the locational and physical aspects of our cities must therefore be conducted in concert with planning for all other programs that governmental and non-governmental agencies conduct."[23] Planning thus now involves the rational and informed use of public power to achieve an extraordinarily wide variety of social and political ends. Law enforcement and the administration of justice have come under the purview of the planners. Neighborhood development and sound community relations are common plannning goals. Planners are involved in the politics of welfare, in responding to social/psychological needs, in stimulating and controlling the urban economy. Indeed, virtually all aspects of social life in the city are now fair game for the planner's drawing board.

The three varieties of innovation—structural, procedural, substantive—have different connotations and, to a great extent, different histories. Each has developed under a separate set of circumstances. Yet, we are justified in grouping them together for at least two reasons. First, their development has been mutually reinforcing. Success in changing the structures of city government, for example, has helped encourage procedural reforms. Similarly, the professionalization and bureaucratization of urban politics has provided an impetus for substantive innovation. Thus, the various histories of managerialism have been intertwined. Second, and more importantly, the three varieties of innovation share, to a great extent, a common intellectual background. Each is informed by and reflective of the managerial premises outlined above, premises regarding the public interest, the role of expertise, the function of government, and the like. As a consequence, we may say that together they form a single intellectual/political perspective on urban politics which has been extremely influential and controversial and which thus merits our most serious attention.

Before looking at this perspective in philosophic terms, though, it will first be useful to examine some conventional critiques. These critiques can help us to understand the current status of the managerial perspective and, hopefully, better appreciate the value of a philosophic approach.

Conventional Critiques

In recent years, managerialism has become the repeated target of social critics. This has been so despite the fact that managerial reforms have continued more or less unabated. Indeed, we may say that while the managerial perspective continues to be politically influential, even dominant, it has become, at least in certain circles, intellectually disreputable. Critics, both of the left and the right, have found much that is pernicious in managerialism. Few of their criticisms, however, penetrate to the theoretical core of the managerial perspective.

Perhaps the most basic and widespread criticisms are aimed at managerialism's antipolitical orientation. As indicated above, the managerial perspective decries the usual give-and-take of political life. The processes of conflict, negotiation, and accommodation, so typical of pluralist politics, are said to result in the satisfaction of particular interests at the expense of the public interest. Managerialists seek to replace this process with a truly public-spirited one emphasizing both the expertise and the "cosmopolitanism"—the value-neutrality—of the decisionmaker.

Against this view, critics have repeatedly asserted that such an "apolitical politics" is, in fact, an impossibility. They have contended that it is not feasible to root out particular interest from *any* decisionmaking process, that the public-spirited and personally disinterested manager simply does not exist, and that managerialist politics can therefore be nothing other than a disguised form of politics-as-usual. Stated otherwise, such critics argue that the distinction between "politics" and "administration" is simply a myth.[24] Most of the work along these lines has been concerned to present empirical illustrations of the political nature of putatively nonpolitical processes. Numerous such studies have been published, but two examples will serve to make the point.

The most striking recent case study of the politics of administration is Robert Caro's biography of Robert Moses, *The Power Broker*.[25] Moses was an early leader of New York's reform movement who eventually became one of the state's most powerful political forces. He attained this position of power by virtue of his role as head of a number of special-purpose districts in New York State, most notably the state's Triborough Bridge and Tunnel Authority. Such special districts were, and are, important elements of the municipal reform strategy. They represented the effort to insulate decisionmakers from the muck of politics, to give experts a fairly free hand in designing programs for dealing with largely technical problems such as sewage treatment, mosquito abatement, flood control, and the construction and administration of bridges and tunnels. Robert Moses was just such an expert, dedicated to the role of professional, nonpartisan government. But as Caro shows in great detail, Moses used his power to achieve political, not merely administrative, ends. By virtue of his position, he was able to exert great influence in the determination of a wide range of public policies in New York State, substantive policies relating to housing, land use, taxing and spending, and transportation, among others. As such, he became deeply involved not simply in the *administration* but in the *formulation* of policy. And, in the process, he became an important party politician, influencing numerous patronage and candidate decisions and eventually running for governor himself. Far from being merely a bureaucrat, Moses used his "neutral" position to become a politician in the most general sense of the word.

A similar case comes from the other end of the continent. In their study of San Francisco's Yerba Buena renewal project, Chester Hartman and associates focus on the pivotal role of one M. Justin Herman.[26] Herman was a professional bureaucrat and planner, experienced in federal administration, who in 1959 became head of the powerful San Francisco Redevelopment Agency. Ostensibly a planning unit, this agency in fact had great decisionmaking potential with "broad-ranging political and economic powers reflecting the full authority of the state apparatus."[27] On Hartman's account, Herman utilized this potential to the fullest. Far from being a mere bureaucrat or implementer, he was in fact a political power whose substantive ideas had a great deal of influence. In Hartman's words:

> Herman was a monument-builder who approached his job like a classical entreprenuer. [H]e used every trick, technique and legal loophole that could be mustered, and when established procedures did not work, he devised new methods, stretching the laws when necessary.[28]

Again, such cases help demonstrate the degree to which political considerations can come to dominate the putatively nonpolitical activities of planning and management. Indeed, managers themselves appear to accept this. Ronald O. Loveridge's research on city managers and Michael Vasu's more recent study of professional planners both reveal a certain willingness to go beyond traditional functions and engage in the business of policymaking.[29] But the more general point here concerns the crucial notion of the "public interest." As indicated above, a central tenet of managerialism is the view that there is always a single identifiable public interest separate from, and superior to, more particular or private interests. It is this notion that critics deny. Perhaps the best source in this regard is Alan Altshuler's *The City Planning Process*.[30] Altshuler's research suggests that there may be no identifiable public interest at all, that efforts to articulate such an interest are often based on more or less concealed private interests and that, as a result, many management decisions are at base political decisions of one kind or another. This is an extremely plausible argument which managerialists have had difficulty rebutting.

There is, however, a second general critique which also demands our attention. I refer to the view which argues that managerialism is essentially undemocratic. This argument is made in several ways. For some, managerialism is basically an elitist doctrine, involving decisions made *for* the masses *by* trained experts and technicians. It is a theory of technocracy, government by experts, rather than democracy, government by the people.[31] For others, managerialism, by relying on rationalistic and bureaucratic modes of decisionmaking, tends to be rigid and difficult to influence. Bureaucratic structures, characterized by complex rules and standard operating procedures, help to insulate decisionmakers, thereby making them less sensitive to the legitimate interests of the community and more able to pursue the special needs of their own organization. The result is a policy which responds more to the niceties of plannning and management theory than to real human needs.

Such criticisms are not without merit. They present a considerable challenge to managerialists, one which has not always been successfully met. Nonetheless, in my view they tend to operate at a rather superficial level which, without gainsaying their cogency, limits their impact. The charge that managerialists are "apolitical" presupposes that a pluralistic politics of conflict and negotiation is itself valuable. It may be, however, that pluralism in fact ratifies parochialism at the expense of public-spiritedness, that it is biased in favor of the more advantaged segments of society, and that it frustrates the legitimate goals of rational, comprehensive planning. The notion that managers are as "political" as anyone else ignores the possibility that the "self-interests" of managers may in fact be more benign, or more in tune with the actual public good, than anyone else's. The criticism that managerialism is elitist assumes both that elitism is an evil and that it can be avoided by some other approach to urban government.

In brief, these criticisms have been concerned to show that managerialism does not always work *in practice* as it does *in principle*. As such, they have left "the principle" largely intact. That is, they have failed to confront the underlying assumptions and ideas upon which the managerial moods rests, assumptions and ideas reflective of certain venerable philosophic positions. A truly complete critique would seek to uncover these underlying ideas, demonstrating their intellectual consequences and evaluating their coherence and their plausibility. It is to such a critique that we now turn.

MANAGERIALISM AND EPISTEMOLOGY

The managerial mood is based upon a series of propositions concerning political obligation and the scope of government. These propositions are, in a sense, synonymous with the managerial perspective itself and thus demand our closest attention. However, they are themselves based upon certain prior propositions concerning the nature of man and his relationship to the world in which he lives, and also concerning the form and content of moral thinking. Managerialism cannot be properly understood until these prior propositions are uncovered and explicated. It is with this task, therefore, that we begin.

The question of the nature of man is perhaps the oldest

question of philosophy, and it has been approached in a number of ways. It has been approached in metaphysical terms so that the question is reformulated "What is the essence of man?" or "What does it mean to be human?" or "How does man differ from non-man?" It has also been approached in ethical terms ("What rights do men have by nature?"), in anthropological terms ("What were the earliest men like?"), and in biological, psychological, and even economic terms.

The managerial perspective reflects a rather different approach according to which the question of human nature is fundamentally an epistemological one. The reasoning behind this will become clearer shortly. But at the outset we can emphasize the fact that managerialism rests upon the following propositions: (1) Man is essentially a knowledge-generating creature; (2) an understanding of how man knows and what he can know is sufficient for understanding man himself; and (3) this understanding also tells us much about man's relationship to other men and to the world in which he lives.

In asserting this, I am arguing that ideas of managerialism have their roots in that great period of intellectual ferment known as the Enlightenment. Now, even a brief history of the Enlightenment is certainly not possible or appropriate here. The Enlightenment itself was an exceedingly complex intellectual movement, spanning the several decades from, roughly, the Glorious Revolution to the French Revolution and including such diverse personages as Hume and Helvetius, Jefferson and Diderot, Turgot and Gibbon, to mention but a few. Its exact parameters, both historical and cultural, have been subject to much dispute, as have its specific intellectual properties.

Such diputes will certainly not be addressed in the present essay. Rather, the Enlightenment to be depicted here is necessarily an abstracted one which emphasizes only the basic and common elements of the various Enlightenment thinkers. And of these basic elements, that which seems most crucial is a general attitude of skepticism toward traditional metaphysics. Briefly, among the major philosophers of the eighteenth century one can witness the gradual and ultimate rejection of the medieval view that the world is a meaningful text.

For the premoderns, the world, like a text, is imbued with meaning which is rationally structured and which is discoverable through reason. One can "read" the world, penetrate to its secrets and find therein its essence, its *telos*, and its value. Since man is but a part of this world, his essence, *telos*, and value are equally knowable. The political philosophers of the Enlightenment largely rejected this view. They regarded the transcendent meaningfulness of the world, and indeed all such transcendent truths, as being either fictitious or, at best, unknowable. The world is no longer seen to be a text but is, rather, more like a machine, the operations of which can be recorded with much precision but the essence of which, the driving principle of which, can only remain a mystery. Such a view, of course, applies also to man himself. If the essence of the world can only be a mystery, then the essence of man must also be an impenetrable secret.

This very premise, though seemingly skeptical and pessimistic, does however point to one fairly certain fact about man, a fact upon which an entire theory of man could be based, quite an optimistic theory at that. This fact is that man does generate something he calls "knowledge." Exactly *what* he can really know, if anything, or *how* he can know it, may be open to considerable dispute. But in the absence of any reliable information about the essence of man, a focus on man's knowledge-generating activities—on epistemology—must suffice. This, however, may not be so bad. For if we can figure out what it is that men claim to "know," then perhaps we can determine the nature of human consciousness, the sources of human ideas, the causes of human behavior. And if we can figure these things out, then perhaps we can develop a good sense of how man is related to the world in which he finds himself. It is, therefore, to epistemology that we must turn for a managerialist theory of man.

Since the time of the Enlightenment, advocates of planning and rational management have been positivists. They have believed that human knowledge can only be *of* sense objects, of positive phenomena, and can only be *through* sense perception, through observation and measurement.[32] Such a view can be found (to a greater or lesser degree, of course) in virtually all managerial thinkers, from Helvetius, Bentham, and Comte to the contemporary theorists of rational planning.

If there is a single philosophic principle which distinguishes positivism, and which unites these historically diverse thinkers, it concerns the relationship between subject and object. In brief, for positivists the knowing subject and object known are considered to be separate and mutually autonomous. Each has an existence, a given reality, that is independent of the other. What this means, among other things, is that the world "out there" is complete as it stands; it is self-subsistent and whole, just waiting to be observed, systematized, and manipulated, though its "meaning" cannot be known.

At least two alleged consequences of this demand our immediate attention. To begin with, for positivists the methods of the natural sciences—rigorous observation and measurement, experimentation in controlled circumstances, the validation or falsification of testable hypotheses—are a model for all inquiry. The human or social sciences are, in principle, no different from the so-called hard sciences and thus ought to proceed in the same fashion. Human behavior, social interaction, psychological motivation—such things are reducible to measurable phenomena which can be analyzed into lawlike propositions much like the lawlike propositions of physics.

This emulation, in fact glorification, of science can be readily found in all managerialists. Indeed, the beginnings of the managerial mood in the Enlightenment coincided with, and were closely influenced by, a growing love affair with natural science, especially physics. For example, eighteenth-century French intellectual life was fairly obsessed with the towering figure of Newton. In Carl Becker's words:

> Newton, more than any other man, had banished mystery from the world by discovering a "universal law of nature," thus demonstrating, what others had only asserted, that the universe was rational and intelligible through, and capable, therefore, of being subdued to the uses of men. The "Newtonian philosophy" was, accordingly, as familiar to common men in the middle eighteenth century as the "Darwinian philosophy" is in our day.[33]

However, it was not merely Newton himself but also the intellectual habits he represented that so intrigued the philosophers of the eighteenth century. Their writings, and those of their heirs, attest time and again to the attractions of the scientific method and to its apparent usefulness for the study of society. As Condorcet put it, the "social art" is a "true science founded, like all other sciences, on facts, experiment, reasoning, and calculation; susceptible, like all others, of an indefinite progress and development, and becoming more useful the more widely its true principles are spread."[34]

This same reverence for science can be readily perceived among contemporary managerialists. Planning is identified today as "the application of scientific method—however crude—to policy-making. . . . Planning is what planning agencies do, i.e., bring scientific advice to bear on decisions concerning policies."[35] The qualified planner is one who can "use the most advanced techniques of data collection and processing and of decision-making and testing."[36] It is through planning that "the findings of the social sciences are being fed into practice settings."[37] Indeed, "contemporary planning education reflects this conception of the planner-as-scientist in its emphasis on statistics, planning methods, and the substantive theories of economics, sociology, regional science, and the other positive social sciences."[38]

This view can be found even today among those planners who seemingly reject the central ideas of traditional planning theory. I am thinking especially of the so-called advocacy planners. In a very real sense, advocacy planners reject many basic tenets of mainstream planning. They tend to be rather less sanguine about the prospects for truly rational planning, more sensitive to the political, psychological, and social obstacles that invariably confront the planner, and much more willing to rely upon the preferences and judgments of the common man.[39] Nonetheless, virtually all advocacy planners, properly understood, ultimately share a basic faith in science and in the epistemological principles implied therein. While they generally disagree with mainstream planners about the way in which the scientific method should be employed, they nonetheless fully agree that the scientific method is the best and only sensible way to consider questions of social policy. It is, after all, this fact that makes them "planners."[40]

Indeed, it can be argued further that without such a view of science the managerial perspective would be nonsensical. Management depends upon the notion that the social world can be observed, systematized, and manipulated like the physical world. If this were not the case, if the world were unknowable or uncontrollable, then "management" would be impossible. It would be, at best, merely the pragmatic and intuitive activity of the prudent statesman or, at worst, an aimless, idle, and unproductive charade. If one cannot systematize human behavior, then one cannot manipulate it; and if one cannot manipulate, one cannot manage.

A second and related theoretical consequence of the subject-object separation is the belief—the often passionate, committed, and unbounded belief—in human progress. According to managerialists, man's lot is improving all the time and will, without much doubt, continue to do so. Of course, science is the force behind this progress. Since its findings are cumulative, the knowledge it generates is ever more certain and ever more comprehensive. Once its methods are emulated by the human sciences, social progress will surely follow. Indeed, the astounding success achieved by the natural sciences can, in time, be matched by those who study and seek to manage society, provided they adopt the principles of the scientific method.

It was Condorcet, more than any other Enlightenment figure, who announced this philosophy of progress. Indeed, Condorcet is fairly exultant:

> And now at last we can exclaim: *truth has conquered: the human race is saved!* Each century will add new enlightenment to that of the century that has preceded it, and this progress, which nothing can henceforth halt or delay, will have no other limits than that of the duration of the universe.[41]

For Condorcet, every scientific advance, based on "ever more comprehensive methods," is a "benefit for humanity." It improves government and education,[42] contributes to the perfection of the arts,[43] and even, ultimately, makes men more virtuous.[44] There is, further, no limit to this progress; man is infinitely perfectible through science.[45] And while Condorcet is certainly an extreme case, his views nonetheless reflect the general faith and optimism of the Enlightenment and its heirs.

Of course, this same belief in progress can be found in the writings of the contemporary managerialists. They have placed their faith largely in the rise of an empirical social science, based on sophisticated quantitative techniques, which presumably can predict human behavior with a high degree of accuracy. This social science provides planners with more and better opportunities to improve the quality of urban life in America. In the words of one important planning theorist, Melvin Webber, "we are acquiring the conceptual and technical competence to undertake comprehensive policy planning. . . . to predict systematically the kinds, scales, and distributions of benefits and costs that various public programs generate."[47] Webber admits, of course, that we will "always lack perfect knowledge." Nonetheless, the outlook for the future is, to say the least, encouraging:

> Improved data systems will permit planners continuously to meter the states of affairs of various population groups, the economy, the municipal fisc, the physical plant, and other aspects of the city. Improved theory, describing and explaining the processes of city life and city growth, will permit us more sensitively to identify those crucial points of public intervention that are appropriate to accomplishing specified objectives.[48]

Indeed, according to Webber there is every reason to believe that the effectiveness of management will increase, and this largely because of the greater attention paid to that "large body of theory and method that has been accumulating in the social and behavioral sciences over the decades.[49]

Again, this belief in progress is presumably traceable to the philosophic separation of subject and object. The discreteness and tangibility of the world "out there"—its identifiability—is necessary if that world is to be appropriated and manipulated. Human behavior itself must be isolated and identified; it must be unambiguously observed and measured if it is to be effectively managed and directed. For if the world were elusive, if we could not pin it down and identify it unambiguously, then we could hardly hope to control it. If the object is *not* a separate entity to be manipulated for human ends, then the simple managerial relationship between subject and object—between the planner and his environment—would be untenable. And, as suggested above, this positivist separation of subject and object is by no means self-evident. Most especially, the independence and self-subsistence of the object of knowledge is open to much dispute. It was Kant, himself a product of the Enlightenment, who first questioned these empiricist assumptions, and who began thereby an entire line of thought the consequences of which are utterly inimical to the managerial mood.[50]

At the risk of oversimplifying, we may suggest that Kant sought to steer a middle course between traditional metaphysicians on the one hand and the emergent positivists on the other. Against the metaphysicians, Kant agreed that we can have no knowledge of the "thing-in-itself," i.e., of those unobservable "essences" to which philosophers from the pre-Socratics to Descartes claimed to have access. In this sense, Kant was certainly something of an empiricist. However, against Hume and the positivists in general, he argued that subject and object are, in a fundamental sense, *not* separated. Specifically, in Kant's view the identity and (for all practical purposes) reality of the object is importantly dependent upon the activity of the subject. The argument, much simplified, goes something as follows: the ultimate truth of the objects "out there" in the world is unknowable; such an ultimate truth is metaphysical—unobservable or, in Kant's terminology, "noumenal"—hence beyond our ken. What we can know are only appearances, the "phenomenal." But all appearances are filtered through and shaped by the activity of the mind. Our mind has, we must deduce, certain categories of understanding—space and time, for example—which help to order and organize our sense experience. Indeed, without such mental categories, the phenomenal world would presumably be chaotic and nonsensical; our observation would be uninterpretable. One possible implication of this view is that the meaningful reality of the world is, in part, created by the mind. We humans—perceiving and thinking beings—actually *constitute* the truth of the world. The facticity of the object—its shape and meaning and its relationship to other objects—is imposed upon it by the activity of the mind, of the human subject. The object is thus *dependent upon* and constituted by the knowing subject.

This *constitutivist* theory, perhaps attributable to Kant, was soon extended and radicalized. Kant's great heir, Hegel, took the first step in this radicalization by historicizing the principle of constitution. For Hegel, different historical periods organize phenomena in different ways; the truth of one era is not the truth of another.[51] Hegel was no relativist; he thought that there was an ultimate reality which was, furthermore, knowable through reason. Nonetheless, his work, along with Kant's, inspired an entire epistemological tradition which emphasizes the historical dependence of facts. For writers in this tradition, sense objects have no meaningful reality apart from the socially-located, ideologically conditioned orientations or world views of those who observe them. All knowledge, all "truth," is relative to social and historical circumstances.[52]

This attack on positivism has been especially important for the social sciences. A host of thinkers have argued that social reality is not composed of objective, positive phenomena; rather, it is made up of meaningful and purposive actions requiring not merely observation but interpretation and understanding.[53] According to such a view, the standard "scientific" approach to the social world is both inappropriate and, indeed, a self-delusion. But even many philosophers of *natural* science have been concerned to revise the standard positivist view. For them, even the hardest of the so-called hard sciences are historically relative, dependent upon sociologically generated viewpoints not reducible to raw empirical observations. The conventional understanding of the scientific method is therefore based on myth and wishful thinking.

The implications of this attack on positivism are deeply incompatible with the assumptions of the managerial mood. To begin with, the very notion of progress becomes dubious, even absurd. Indeed, it has become rather fashionable to ridicule the idea of human progress, to find in it a naive and implausible view of history. The argument was made first and perhaps most strikingly by Rousseau, one of the earliest and most brilliant critics of the Enlightenment. In his masterful "Discourse on the Arts and Sciences" Rousseau was at his provocative, inflammatory best, claiming that the morals of society decay in direct proportion to the advance of the arts and sciences.[55] The rise of science as a general social practice produces, among other things, a taste for luxury, a penchant for idleness, a preoccupation with self-interest, and a kind of slavish sociability. The real virtues of man, e.g., courage, discipline, and industry, fail to satisfy a world that has become blasé, mannered, and sophisticated. In place of these real virtues we find the mere appearance of virtue. Rousseau's point is that progress may not be what it seems to be, and in this he has been followed by a host of thinkers, from a radical anarchist like Georges Sorel to a contemporary conservative such as Michael Oakeshott.[56]

Perhaps even more to the point, by emphasizing the historical relativity of social scientific understanding, critics of positivism have cast grave doubts on the neutrality and objectivity so highly valued by managerialists. If judgments of fact inevitably reflect position and perspective, if the findings of "science" are unavoidably influenced by such extrascientific factors, then the image of the dispassionate, apolitical manager— the bureaucrat, the city manager, the comprehensive planner— becomes absurd indeed. There is no Archimedean point, no special position from which the manager can gain purchase on urban problems. Hence, the manager's "knowledge"—the knowledge based on empirical social science—cannot in any obvious way be privileged. And indeed, if there is no disinterested social science in the classic sense, then there is probably no management in the classic sense.

MANAGERIALISM AND UTILITY

These problems, which pertain to managerial assumptions about the nature of man as a knowledge-generating creature, lead directly to further problems which pertain to moral theory in general. The epistemological positions upon which managerialism is based have crucial implications for ethics which reveal perhaps more clearly the political biases inherent in the managerial mood.

There are at least two moral positions typically associated with positivism. The first of these concerns the separation of facts and values. In brief, according to positivists, "facts"—that is, the objects of sense perception or "positive phenomena"—can be unambiguously known. We can reliably distinguish, without problem, red from blue, big from small, political participation from nonparticipation, and the like. More particularly, our assertions about facts can be tested and adjudged correct or incorrect. That is, the assertion "Republicans are more likely to vote than Democrats" is a hypothesis, the truth of which can be simply determined by marshaling empirical evidence. One merely observes the voting behavior of Republicans and Democrats, records and tabulates these observations, and arrives at findings which tend either to confirm or disconfirm the initial hypothesis. No such method exists concerning values. According to positivists, assertions about values can only be statements of preference; hence, they can have no objective validity. The statement "Chicken tastes better than steak" really means "I like chicken more than steak"; and while the defender of chicken can certainly try to make arguments in behalf of his preference (e.g., chicken is more nutritious, is a better value, has a finer texture, is more popular, etc.), ultimately the question of which tastes better is a personal one in which there is, and can be, no intersubjective right or wrong. One can adduce no evidence that would clearly support one's preference. Thus, values cannot be tested; empirical evidence cannot, of itself, discriminate between good or bad. There are no absolute or definitive moral truths.[57]

It took some time for the early managerialists to reach this conclusion. For many theorists of the Enlightenment, right and wrong were sufficiently self-evident that the problem of moral knowledge did not loom very large. Indeed, some of these theorists regarded morals as perfectly amenable to scientific analysis. Helvetius, for example, saw the "propositions in morality, politics and metaphysics becoming as susceptible of demonstration as the propositions of geometry."[58] Gradually, however, the logic of the positivist position forced the ultimate realization that neither Newton's science nor anything like it could of itself distinguish moral right from wrong. (Indeed, it also forced the realization, unacknowledged by those like Helvetius, that the propositions of geometry were logical, not empirical.) It was perhaps David Hume, more than anyone else, who made this realization explicit and gave it the status of a philosophic principle. For Hume, morality is essentially non-rational; one cannot, in the end, distinguish between good passions and bad passions. One can use reason and science to choose the best means for achieving a particular end, but one cannot use them to select the best end. It is in this sense that reason "is and ought only to be the slave of the passions and can never pretend to any other office than to serve and obey them."[59]

Here we have a classic statement of the separation of facts and values. Its consequences are several. First of all, it implies a rejection of higher moral laws. Morality is not something to be discovered, as one "discovers" the Law of God or the Laws of Nature or even the laws of physical motion. It is, rather, a mere preference which must in some sense be invented or posited and then imposed on others. Further, the fact-value dichotomy implies that science must therefore restrict itself to the assessment of means, not ends. Science is powerless to tell us what we ought to do. It can, of course, tell us the consequences of potential courses of action. But ultimately, an "ought" can never be derived from an "is."

Finally, and most importantly, the separation of facts and values means that morality can only be conventional and must probably be utilitarian. Again, it was Hume who drew this conclusion most clearly. To begin with, if questions of moral right or wrong are simply matters of inclination, then systems of morality—i.e., generally accepted standards of ethical conduct—can only be products of conventional human decisions. Morality is therefore man-made. Humans in society compare their tastes, inclinations, and passions and, more or less tacitly, agree upon acceptable notions of right and wrong. Such notions, then, are not discovered, they are created; they are not natural, but artificial. But further, we must ask on what grounds, and from what motives, are such moral constructs derived. According to most positivists, history, reason, and common sense all point to one simple and definitive answer: utility. As Sabine writes:

> The conventions of society may be explained by history or psychology or anthropology but they cannot claim validity in

any but the relative sense of being generally convenient and in accord with men's estimate of utility.[60]

This is a crucial implication. Postivism, as an epistemological position, is often thought to imply an ethics of utilitarianism. Such a conclusion means two things. First, it means that social policy ought to strive for the maximum gratification of individual desires. If good and bad are relative to individual inclinations, then the more such inclinations are gratified the more "useful" and effective is the policy. Second, it means that "right" and "justice" are entirely dependent on consequences. Something is morally right only if its consequences are good, i.e., only if it maximizes utility.

Virtually all managerialists are utilitarians who also believe in the fact-value dichotomy. Indeed, utilitarianism is a natural way of dealing with the problems posed by that dichotomy. That is, in the face of the unknowability of moral "facts," the most convenient recourse is to the real, empirical preferences and desires of individuals or groups of individuals; utilitarianism takes these preferences and desires as they are, without prejudice, and merely seeks to maximize them; it does so by rationally and scientifically determining the most efficient and effective distribution of resources so as to achieve the greatest good for the greatest number. In this way, the strategy of utilitarianism almost amounts to deriving an "ought" (the greatest good) from an "is" (the actual preferences of groups or individuals). In the words of Helvetius, "every moral truth is nothing more than a method of increasing or securing the happiness of the majority."[61]

Such a strategy was adopted by virtually all of the classic managerialists, from Condorcet and Bentham to Comte and Karl Mannheim. And indeed, this same general notion can be found equally in the contemporary managerialist literature. To pick just one example, in their important essay on planning theory, Davidoff and Reiner write of facts and values as follows:

> Verification of facts and verification of values involve different techniques. The definition of a fact requires the possibility of disproving the assertion. [But] we can speak of verification of

values only in terms of their consistency with values of a higher level. Eventually there must be reference to ultimate values which are essentially assumed and asserted as postulates.[62]

From this they conclude that the decisionmaker should not be in the business of making value judgments. Rather, his function is merely utilitarian, i.e., to identify the "distribution of values among people,"[63] select the best means for maximizing those values,[64] and seek to "effectuate" those means so as to achieve the most efficient and useful policy.[65]

The implications of such a position for urban politics are both crucial and controversial and will be treated in the next section of this chapter. As a purely ethical position, however, it does have certain philosophic difficulties which require at least some consideration. Both the fact-value dichotomy and, more broadly, utilitarianism have been subjected to considerable criticism of late which, in itself, raises serious questions about the cogency of the managerial mood in general.

The fact-value dichotomy has been rejected on at least two related grounds:

1. To begin with, some have argued that the dichotomy is simply a myth and that there is no such thing as a value-free social science. The milder form of this position was suggested by Max Weber, who argued that through the very selection of research topics values intrude on the social scientific enterprise.[66] According to Weber, the nearly infinite complexity of the social world requires that the social scientist be selective; but for that very reason, the principle of selection cannot itself be based on social science. It must, instead, derive from the cultural, value-laden contexts in which the social scientist operates. The stronger form of the argument is to be found, for example, in Charles Taylor's fine article on "Neutrality in Political Science."[67] According to Taylor, values impinge not merely in the selection of topics for study but, more importantly, in the selection of theoretical perspectives. For Taylor, all social scientific theories involve the specification of one or another "dimension of variation." Each such dimension defines the research problem in a particular way; each details the kinds of variables that will be relevant in addressing that problem; and each is itself based upon, and utterly inseparable

from, various normative considerations. Thus, no theory is value-neutral; all social science carries with it the excess baggage of morality. From this, incidentally, Taylor does not conclude that social scientific theories cannot be compared and evaluated vis-á-vis one another. For in his view, and against the so-called emotivist position in ethics, Taylor contends that there is a fundamental difference between statements of mere preference and moral statements. Preferences, being solely expressions of taste and inclination, cannot, it is true, be objectively assessed and evaluated. But moral judgments are, by definition, based on reasons. When one takes a moral position, as opposed to merely stating a perference, one is thereby claiming to be able to adduce defensible grounds in support of that position, grounds which can in principle be discussed and adjudged adequate or inadequate. Taylor's view is, thus, twofold: (a) there can be no value-free social science, and (b) nonetheless, values can, in a sense, be verified. Both positions are incompatible with the managerial ideology.

2. The second general critique of the fact-value dichotomy is even more radical. It contends that the separation of facts and values is itself a value-*inspired* rather than merely value-*laden* move, one that has tremendous political overtones. Crucial in this regard are the writings of George Lukács and his followers in the so-called Frankfurt school of critical theory, including Theodore Adorno, Max Horkheimer, Herbert Marcuse, and, more recently, Jürgen Habermas.[68] For such writers, the fact-value dichotomy is a unique and important part of the so-called liberal bourgeois ideology, and serves to protect and maintain the status quo. By emphasizing the verifiability of facts and the nonverifiability of values, the dichotomy suggests in effect that dominant and established concepts of right and justice, for example those of capitalism, cannot be subjected to rigorous and decisive critiques. Of course, we can say that we do not like particular social arrangements or particular distributive schemes; but beyond that there is nothing we can say. To accept the fact-value dichotomy, therefore, is to renounce the possibility of *proving* the evils of the status quo, of demonstrating clearly and definitively the injustice of, say, its distributive consequences. Moral arguments, including radical criticisms of capitalist

society, lose their scientific status and, as a consequence, their sense of legitimacy and force.

These critiques of the fact-value dichotomy are, in my view, quite substantial and present real problems for the managerial ideology. But more broadly, the moral utilitarianism upon which managerialism rests has itself been subject to serious questions which deserve some notice here. Again, the central figure in this regard is probably Kant, whose influence in the realm of modern moral theory rivals, and perhaps surpasses, his importance in the realm of epistemology.[69] Kant's critique of utilitarianism is radical, thoroughgoing, and quite profound. His view, stated in the parlance of meta-ethics, is that all forms of utilitarianism are "teleological." This means that they base judgments of right and wrong solely in terms of consequences. Teleological theories define "right" as nothing more than the maximization of some previously specified and philosophically underived preference or value.[70] One problem with such theories, according to Kant, is that they offer no basis for deciding whether the preference or value to be maximized is legitimate or not. Presumably, for teleologists anything we desire is acceptable, provided that desire can be gratified without compromising some other, more important desire. But it can be argued that many of our desires, even those easily gratified, are not especially estimable or are perhaps even perverse. Further, it can be shown that the gratification of any desire often entails costs, the acceptability of which cannot be judged on purely teleological grounds. Thus, utilitarianism seems to ignore the question of moral action itself and thereby fails to tackle the most essential issues of ethical theory. In response to this, Kant proposed an alternative approach which moral theorists have classified as "deontological." According to deontological theories, right can and must be determined independent of consequences. It is the nature of the action itself that counts. This means that ends are never sufficient to justify means; actions must be inherently, intrinsically right or wrong. Of course, Kant's formulation along these lines is too complex to explicate here. In brief, he emphasized the *process* by which decisions are made, rather than the content of such decisions. If one decides on the basis of an authentic and rational decisionmaking process, a process which considers questions of principle and which treats other humans as ends in themselves rather than as means, then one's actions are likely to be morally defensible.

Such a view provides a real alternative to the kind of simple managerial utilitarianism outlined above; it places a premium less on efficiency and expertise, less on the "product," than on the qualities of the moral agent himself, on the "process." The upshot is that the managerial mood is based upon a set of moral postulates which are, at the least, open to question. Without the fact-value dichotomy, and without utilitarianism, the managerial perspective would lack any moral foundation or claim to legitimacy. If definitive moral judgments *are* possible, if we *can* reliably assess ends without exclusive reference to means, then the indispensability of the rational manager might be seriously compromised.

MANAGERIALIST POLITICS

In my judgment, the criticisms outlined thus far are substantial indeed. Moreover, it must be remembered that managerialism is fundamentally an intellectual movement, an ideology based on certain philosophic principles. Its cogency as a set of ideas and, hence, the cogency of its institutional recommendations are heavily dependent upon the degree to which those principles are themselves persuasive and sound. The council-manager system, civil service, metro-reform, the professionalization of government—these things are not self-validating. Their legitimacy, rather, is based upon the legitimacy of the managerial ideology that underlies them. If that ideology is shown to be in some sense unsound or unpersuasive, then the political forms and practices it prescribes either cannot be defended or must be defended on wholly different grounds.

Managerialism has been a powerful and extremely influential ideology for the past two centuries. It has been in tune with a culture increasingly absorbed by the preoccupations and promises of science. It has served as the politically and socially oriented concomitant of a general movement of ideas that has adopted, for various reasons, a positivist epistemology and a utilitarian ethics. While this movement has, in the past, produced its "grand treatises," and one thinks here of the works of Condorcet, Comte, St.-Simon, and Bentham, among others, I know of no contemporary writing that presents an equivalently broad and sophisticated defense of managerialist ideas. Nonetheless, managerialism remains the dominant ideology of American urban politics. Its influence is to be found not only in the current practice of city government, but also in the countless theoretical essays and monographs on planning theory produced by practitioners and academics alike. A number of these have been cited above, but one of the best statements I know of is an essay by Donald Michael entitled "Urban Policy in the Nationalized Society." This was the lead article for an important symposium on "process planning" in the *American Institute of Planners Journal;* as such, it can stand as a useful exemplar of the contemporary managerialist literature.[71]

All of the characteristic elements of managerialism are present in Michael's work. He is, to begin with, extraordinarily optimistic about the future of planning and the benefits it can provide. For him, the day is near when social planning will begin to "demonstrate its capacity to smooth social transitions and operations."[72] This will be the result of increasingly "sophisticated techniques" which can be used to analyze and evolve programs for dealing with major urban problems. Thus, the outlook for Michael is extremely encouraging:

> [We] can expect very substantial increases in the knowledge needed to understand and manipulate society and to alter its institutions. . . . Such knowledge will significantly increase our ability to effect social change and thereby increase our capacity to rationalize many programs and projects.[73]

In this optimism, this belief in progress, we can also see where Michael's values lie. For him, our hope, as well as our destiny, is the increased rationalization of social policy and processes. There are a variety of factors here pushing or pulling us toward a rationalized society. Among these are the greater complexity and scale of urban social problems, the resulting need for "long lead-time planning," the alleged shortage of "top-flight professionals" which will force more effective forms of organization, and the general "increases in knowledge" that come from the increased application of the scientific method. It is true, says Michael, that certain other factors may impede progress:

> [It] is worth reemphasizing that there will be men and institutions opposing the trend toward increasing rationalization of the urban condition. There will be those who have a deep emotional commitment as well as a practical interest in continuing to operate in less rationalized ways. The newer approaches will necessarily disrupt status and empires and even as now, rationalization will be fought, often bitterly.74

Ultimately, though, these fights will be won. The forces of light will emerge victorious. Rationalization will become a way of life.

Again, this is both our destiny and our hope. For Michael, rationalization denotes an enlightened, effective, and altogether proper approach to the social problems of urban areas. Indeed, the complexity of such problems absolutely requires the "assiduous application of rationalization techniques."75 These techniques will ensure the development of long lead-time planning, so necessary in a world of growing complexity and urbanization. They will also ensure the prominence of experts and scientists, whose characteristics—both technical *and* temperamental—make them highly suitable for positions of policy leadership.76 Finally, they will create the intellectual and institutional contexts conducive to the twin goals of efficiency and effectiveness.

Here we have managerialism in all its particulars: the emphasis on science and progress, on rationalization and positivism, on the maximization of utility as a social goal. And we can also discover, at least implicit in Michael's work, the central *political* principles of the managerial mood. Specifically, Michael's ideas suggest an emphasis on social control as the essence of political life. According to Michael, the rise of social science will make it possible to manipulate society, to effect social change in desired directions.77 It will permit planners to combine large numbers of variables so as to better simulate, predict, and shape human behavior. This, in turn, will necessitate the increasing centralization of "decision making, planning and operations management" and the "inexorable expansion of the federal government."[78] The result will be a system more adept at social control, better able to produce an efficient, smoothly running society. Of course, Michael is aware of at least some of the dangers involved. The technocrats who will presumably plan for us must be possessed of special wisdom and moral insight, and be well versed in philosophy, history, theology, and aesthetics. The techniques of rationalization are powerful ones and can be used for good or evil; Michael's planners must be sure that the good wins out. Of course, nowhere does he tell us how these scientists—good positivists and relativists all, we must presume—can possibly claim to know how to discriminate between good and evil. Nonetheless, such dangers are secondary. For the opportunities presented by a social control strategy are so great, potentially so beneficial, that the risks involved must seem rather minor indeed.

Implicit here is a theory of political obligation and a theory of the public realm. For managerialists, obligation is rooted entirely in utilitarian considerations. The individual ought to obey society only as long as society is providing him with tangible benefits. As soon as the polity stops operating in an efficient and effective manner, the individual's obligation would presumably stop. One is never obligated by virtue of consent or convenant, nor by virtue of natural or transcendent ethical laws. Indeed, higher moral considerations play virtually no role at all. Interest alone suffices to justify the claims to obedience that any regime must make.

There are, of course, many serious criticisms of such a notion of political obligation. To begin with, it pays relatively little attention to the kind of deep civic attachment and public-spiritedness which, in the view of some, is the absolute requisite of political society. The managerial view grounds obligation solely in terms of calculations of utility. According to such a perspective, the polity is—at least in principle— reduced to a benefit-generating enterprise in which customary, traditional, and moral attachments are relatively superfluous. But for many theorists it is precisely these latter kinds of attachments, and the sense of duty they imply, that make political society what it is. Indeed, without such a common social bond, regimes have great difficulty demanding obedience and exacting the often unpleasant contributions that the public interest typically requires.[79]

Even more importantly, the managerialist theory of obligation makes it difficult to distinguish good regimes from what would generally be considered bad ones. Presumably, it must hold that any government that delivers the "goods" merits our obedience. Thus, authoritarian, plutocratic, even fascist forms of government cannot be ruled out in principle. This is certainly a disturbing consequence. For indeed, some would argue that nondemocratic regimes are in fact likely to be more efficient, hence more productive, than democracies. As a result, democracy typically requires justifications other than those of efficiency and material interest. But the managerialist notion of obligation does not appear to allow for any such judgments regarding the various forms of government. A strict managerialist cannot say that democracy is in principle better than autocracy, that aristocracy is better than depositism, and the like; all he can say is that we should choose the most efficient and productive regime, whatever it happens to be.

Emphatically, my argument is *not* that managerialism is "fascistic" or that it *inevitably* has totalitarian consequences. Indeed, it is certain that most planners in American urban politics genuinely favor one or another form of garden-variety democracy. However, I would maintain that for them to do so requires that they import arguments from *outside* of the managerial ideology. This is, of course, a reasonable and acceptable strategy on their part; I know of no intellectual law that demands total ideological purity. Nonetheless, this very resort to arguments from outside of managerialism clearly suggests the weakness of the ideology itself. For the fact is that the *logic* of managerialism imposes no clear theoretical objections to the most straightforward and complete kind of undemocratic rule. There is nothing in managerialism per se that would rule out authoritarian or even totalitarian political arrangements. As an ideology, managerialism simply invokes standards of efficiency and economy, delivering the goods, maximizing utility. Presumably, then, it can only rule out regimes that fail to perform successfully in terms of these criteria. Other criteria, e.g., humanistic criteria such as freedom, moral autonomy, community, or individual dignity, are at best secondary and at worst irrelevant. According to strict managerial principles, any regime that does deliver the goods merits our obedience.

Implicitly, this theory of obligation is also bound up with a notion of the public realm. In brief, the managerialist perspective is an activist one in which the scope of politics is in principle unlimited. The managerialist considers law not as a restraint on government, a protection against arbitrary or capricious interference, but rather as a tool for government, a means by which behavior can be shaped and directed.[80] Indeed, the criterion of good government is in large part the degree to which behavior is molded and guided in appropriate ways. The scope of the public realm, therefore, is potentially all-encompassing.

This is an implication which can be found in virtually all managerialist theories. From Helvetius's educative society or St.-Simon's regime of scientists, artists, and industrialists to the "rationalized" world of Donald Michael, managerialists have viewed government as an instrument of almost unlimited social control. Understandably, this is an implication which has disturbed critics for the last two centuries.

Some have described managerialist politics as, in effect, an antipolitics, an effort to destroy the commonality, the "publicity" of public or civic life. Sheldon Wolin, for example, describes a "highly diverse group of writers"[81]—from St.-Simon and Fourier to Weber and Mannheim—all of whom stress the need for order and organization, thereby expressing their "contempt for politics."[82] For such writers, organization or bureaucratization is a desirable method of social control providing "a vast hierarchy of authority," antithetical—in Wolin's view—to the give-and-take of real politics.[83] Other critics frankly point to the authoritarian, even totalitarian implications of the managerialist perspective. Robert Nisbet, for example, sees in the increasing rationalization of society the demise of community, hence the demise of any effective barrier to oppressive centralization and despotism.[84]

Both of these criticisms can be found in the prescient writings of Tocqueville. In his long discussion of the New England town, for example, Tocqueville writes glowingly about civic virtue, about the joys and benefits of participation in public affairs. These towns are the "schools of democracy," bastions of liberty, and the true sources of the common good.[85] Their decline, perhaps inevitable, would deal a severe blow to the cause of freedom. And then, in his famous chapter on the kinds of despotism which democracies have to fear, Tocqueville writes hauntingly about the managerialist vision:

> The first thing that strikes the observation is an innumerable multitude of men, all equal and alike, incessantly endeavoring to produce the petty and paltry pleasures with which they glut their lives. Each of them, living apart, is as a stranger to the fate of all the rest. . . . Above this race of men stands an immense and tutelary power, which takes upon itself alone to secure their gratifications and to watch over their fate. That power is absolute, minute, regular, provident, and mild. It would be like the authority of a parent if, like that authority, its object was to prepare men for manhood; but it seeks, on the contrary, to keep them in perpetual childhood; it is well content that the people should rejoice, provided they think of nothing but rejoicing. For their happiness such a government willingly labors, but it chooses to be the sole agent and the only arbiter of that happiness. . . . It covers the surface of society with a network of small, complicated rules, minute and uniform, through which the most original minds and the most energetic characters cannot penetrate, to rise above the crowd. The will of man is not shattered, but softened, bent, and guided; men are seldom forced by it to act, but they are constantly restrained from acting. Such a power does not destroy, but it prevents existence; it does not tyrannize, but it compresses, enervates, extinguishes, and stupefies a people, till each nation is reduced to nothing better than a flock of timid and industrious animals, of which the government is the shepherd.[86]

The practical consequences of managerialism are by no means necessarily authoritarian. But the ideology, in its pure form, provides no argument against such consequences. And it is in partial response to this fact that other approaches to the urban crisis have been developed, approaches which promise a more democratic and humane strategy for dealing with the problems of our cities.

3. COMMUNITY AND PARTICIPATION

The term *community action* has become an integral part of the vocabulary of urban politics. Even today, long after the demise of the War on Poverty, the connotations of community action remain very much alive—negative connotations for some, positive for others, but provocative for the study of urbanism in general. Indeed, while the Community Action Program itself is quite dead, its impact is still strongly felt in virtually all major American cities.

What I wish to focus on is a curious yet decisive change that the term *community action* underwent rather early in its career. As is well known, in 1960 and 1961 the Ford Foundation, long active in urban affairs, sought a new approach to the problems of our cities, one which would avoid the very serious shortcomings associated with such earlier programs as urban renewal and public housing. These latter actually appeared to have worsened rather than improved the lot of the urban poor. Urban renewal had rebuilt many central business districts, but in so doing had merely displaced the inner-city poor, forcing them to move from one marginal area to another. Public housing had institutionalized ghetto life, and had done so, according to critics, in an especially insensitive, dehumanizing way. A new approach was needed which would focus effectively and systematically on the most serious of our urban problems.

The approach adopted by the Ford Foundation was embodied in the so-called Gray Areas Projects, and it is here that we can locate the beginnings of "community action." A few characteristics of the Gray Areas Projects are especially salient.[1] First, they sought to focus not on cities but on neighborhoods within cities, neighborhoods located in those deteriorating gray areas that lie between the central business district and the suburbs.

Second, these neighborhoods were to be treated as though each were, in some sense, a sociopolitical system in its own right—a "community" the residents of which suffered many of the same problems for many of the same reasons, and who shopped at the same stores, were represented by the same politicians, sent their children to the same schools, dealt with the same police precinct, and the like. Finally, the Gray Areas Projects operated on the premise that problems such as poverty and delinquency required a systematic revamping of neighborhood life. The problem of juvenile delinquency, for example, could not be solved by treating only the delinquents themselves. Rather, delinquency was seen to be part of a complex neighborhood social system involving the family, economic opportunities, public education, culture, the physical enviroment, and so on. Thus, in order to deal with delinquency one had to be prepared to reshape the entire life of a community, to create a social and political environment conducive to the development of healthy, socially productive individuals. This kind of broad and radical approach, focusing on the intertwined gamut of neighborhood ills, acquired the name community action.

Though political factors certainly played their role in the development of the Gray Areas Projects, the notion of community action was not simply a product of political bargaining and compromise. It was, rather, an intellectual construct developed by academically and professionally trained thinkers in the Public Affairs Department of the Ford Foundation. As such, community action represented a prime example of what was termed in the previous chapter substantive innovation. Perhaps never in the history of urban America had there been so audacious and sweeping a notion of social engineering. Physically, of course, the Gray Areas Projects were quite limited in scope, focusing on a few selected neighborhoods in a few selected cities. Their actual fiscal impact was also comparatively modest. But the ideas themselves were virtually uncontainable. They involved an effort to entirely remake the social and even personal lives of a community of individuals, to use our scientific knowledge of the causes of poverty and despair in order to eliminate those conditions. They were based on the notion that one could restructure the community economic system, plan a new school curriculum, reorganize the delivery of social services, and adjust the neighborhood political apparatus in a way that would ultimately destroy the cycle of poverty. They expressed, finally, the Enlightenment ideal that expertise and scientific research could be utilized to improve the lot of those who, caught up as they were in that cycle of poverty, were unable to help themselves.

The success or failure of the Gray Areas Projects is a subject of much dispute. What is indisputable, however, is that they were enormously influential, and that their influence manifested itself most decisively in the community action provisions of the War on Poverty. But perhaps paradoxically, it was here, in the War on Poverty itself and in the ways in which it came to be implemented, that the term community action underwent a decisive change.

As is well known, the phrase *maximum feasible participation* became a crucial and most controversial component of the community action provisions of the War on Poverty. As is also well known, the precise origins of this phrase are obscure, and the purposes it was meant to convey unclear.[2] Two things, however, are clear. First, those who formulated the War on Poverty were operating largely from a managerial perspective. In other words, they were, like the Ford Foundation people, interested in social engineering, in devising a systematic plan to attack a community's cycle of poverty. But second, the very structure of the Community Action Program, and the vagueness of phrases such as maximum feasible participation, created a unique opportunity for those who had a quite different conception of community action itself.

I refer now to those for whom community action meant action *by*, not merely *for*, the community. Such people perhaps agreed that the urban neighborhood was an identifiable and relatively discrete social system comprised of like people facing like problems. They may also have agreed that the etiology of poverty is exceedingly complex, and that the poor are caught up in a web of frustration and despair. But they disagreed as to the solution. In particular, they adopted what we can call a "communalist" perspective. According to such a view, the problems of the urban poor can be best treated not by the planners and bureaucrats but by the poor themselves. Give the poor sufficient social and political resources, give them a fair chance to change things around, and the cycle of poverty can be broken once and for all.

This view came to appropriate the term community action, in theory if not in practice. While many local Community Action Programs never gave real power to the people, the proponents of community action soon came to adopt one or another kind of communalist ideology. And in the post-OEO period, such an ideology came to be embodied in a host of ongoing programs, practices, and institutions including community school boards, community health boards, neighborhood and block associations, community development corporations, neighborhood self-help groups, ad-hoc protest groups, little city halls, community task forces, neighborhood ombudsmen, and the like. Such organizations have become a crucial part of the urban political landscape, introducing new interests and new actors into the decisionmaking process. As such, they have made the communalist perspective a major ideology of contemporary urban politics.

This ideology is, in large part, based on an explicit and pointed rejection of the managerialist view. It emphasizes citizen government at the expense of experts and social engineers. It makes a virtue of localism as opposed to the cosmopolitanism of the managerialists. Perhaps most importantly, it judges not so much the *outcomes* of the political process as the *process* itself. That is, it views democratic government as an end in itself, not merely a means to some other end, and regards any compromise as a potentially destructive and, indeed, unacceptable deviation. This is a populist view, the roots of which lie deep in Western culture. It emphasizes the sociological bases of political life and, in so doing, constitutes a formidable challenge to the dominant interpretations of the urban crisis.

The Communalist Position

The communalist position can be reconstructed in terms of five theses. Each of these is discrete in its own right; each, nonetheless, is bound up with the others so as to form a single, coherent perspective.

1. *Democratic politics means participatory politics.* For communalists, democracy and participation are virtually synonymous: to the degree that full participation is not achieved, the goals of democracy are thereby compromised. This is a more controversial thesis than one might think. It implicitly rejects, for example, the basic premises of Madisonian democracy which was concerned in part to restrain the political power of the masses.[3] It also rejects, at least in principle, representative democracy; to be governed by one's "representatives" is to be denied the opportunity for genuine *self*-government.[4] And finally, it rejects the so-called pluralist interpretation of democracy; a political system dominated by a plurality of hierarchically organized interest groups, all competing with one another in the political marketplace, is merely another variety of elite rule. In opposition to all of these approaches, communalists hold that democracy requires the direct and unvarnished exercise of the power of the people. Anything less is a threat to the democratic principle and an invitation to alienation, exploitation, and tyranny.

2. *Democracy, so defined, can only flourish in communal settings.* The argument is largely sociological. In order for participatory democracy to work, it is necessary that citizens act in terms of the good of the whole, that they are able to empathize with the needs of their neighbors and fellow citizens, and that there is among them a sound basis for agreement concerning political right and wrong. In the absence of such public-spiritedness and consensus, democracy would likely crumble in the face of egoism, competitiveness, and social war. Democracy is thus a fragile thing; it can thrive only in a hospitable social environment. Such an environment is provided by "community," i.e., a variety of social organization characterized by relatively close interpersonal relations and by relatively high levels of political consensus.

3. *Community, so defined, is most characteristic of small, geographically distinct social entities.* The communalist perspective places great emphasis on size. It argues that relatively small units are much more conducive to the development of community than are large units. The smaller the unit, the more its residents are likely to know one another, or know about one another, hence more likely to understand and sympathize with each other's

needs and desires. Large units, on the other hand, tend toward impersonality. They foster selfishness and competitiveness, and thus do not conduce to genuine civic involvement. Much the same arguments are made concerning territoriality. The more clearly defined a geographical unit is, the more likely will its residents develop a sense of community, of common purpose and identity with their neighbors.

4. *Neighborhood government is the most viable form of urban government.* This is, in many ways, a summary of the first three theses. The neighborhood, being small and geographically defined, is the basis of community in our cities; but community itself is the only possible basis of participatory democracy. Hence, if we are interested in democracy for our cities, then we must locate it primarily in the urban neighborhood. Of course, the actual degree to which communalists support devolution of political authority to the neighborhoods varies considerably. At one extreme, there are those who envision the virtual end of municipal government as we know it, who see all or most areas of urban policymaking and service delivery best handled at the neighborhood level. According to such a veiw, neighborhoods ought to run their own schools, enforce the law themselves, maintain their streets, regulate their businesses, plan for land use, and the like. At the other extreme are those who see neighborhood government in an essentially advisory role, articulating local needs and interests to decisionmakers at the municipal, regional, state, or federal level. The differences between these extremes are obviously crucial. Nonetheless, communalists of all stripes are agreed on the importance of the neighborhood and its role in the maintenance and enhancement of urban democracy.

5. *The political process is, at base, a means for generating and articulating the public's will.* Stated otherwise, the purpose of politics is to create a context in which individuals can come together, deliberate, and decide in a truly public-spirited way issues of public concern. The emphasis is thus on the *process*, rather than the *product*, of politics. To be sure, the substance of public policy is important. Indeed, our choices regarding the raising and spending of money, the allocation of rights and duties, the distribution of goods and services, and the like—these are clearly the hallmark choices of politics. But for

communalists, even more important is the *way* in which we choose. Do we decide in a manner that alienates large segments of society, that frustrates the participatory impulse, that conduces to political egoism, isolation, and withdrawal? Or do we decide in a manner that taps the energies of everyone, that fosters the development of civic involvement, that ennobles those who partake in the deliberation of public ends? For communalists, this is the crucial issue. And it is in response to this issue that they have opted for participatory neighborhood government—grassroots democracy in an urban setting.

This last thesis shows, perhaps more clearly than the others, the degree to which communalism stands in direct opposition to the managerial mood. For managerialists, the product is everything. The optimal use of resources, the efficient and equitable distribution of benefits, the general spread of prosperity, in short the maximization of utility—these are the criteria with which to judge the political process. And given such criteria, the value of community, participation, even democracy itself would seem to be negotiable. If participatory democracy, for example, conduces to the maximization of utility, however defined, then it has value; but if not, then it ought to have no peremptory hold on us.

For communalists, on the other hand, the democratic process is an end in itself. Indeed, characterized by civic virtue and a commitment to the common good, the genuine democratic citizen is a noble creature, one who has achieved a dignity and a sense of self-respect sufficient to outweigh any managerial calculations of utility. This then is an enticing moral view, a powerful political ideology which echoes in our history and which now leads the call for neighborhood government and community power.

COMMUNALISM IN AMERICA

The tradition of community democracy is as venerable as any American political tradition. Its roots can be traced in certain of the early Colonial settlements, especially those of Williams in Rhode Island and the Quakers in Pennsylvania. The Mayflower Compact itself, with its voluntarist, contractarian elements, would seem to be implicitly populist. And while the degree to which actual grassroots democracy has been practiced in the United States is open to some dispute, it is clear that the communalist ideology has played an important role in our history.

If there is a single definitive source on community democracy in the nineteenth century, it must surely be Tocqueville's *Democracy in America*, most notably the famous passages on the New England town. Not only does Tocqueville provide a vivid image of how town democracy operated in the early nineteenth century, he also offers a defense of community government that can stand as a basic statement of American democratic communalism, despite its being written by a Frenchman of distinctly aristocratic origins and tastes.

In America Tocqueville found townships to possess a rare degree of political vitality. He partly attributed this to the unique political position of American local governments. By virtue of their relative autonomy, these governments could command active loyalty from their citizens. Tocqueville wrote of the citizen that

> he obeys society. . . . because he acknowledges the utility of an association with his fellow men. [W]ithout power and independence a town may contain good subjects, but it can have no active citizens. . . . The native of New England is attached to his township because it is independent and free.[5]

Such passages are in a liberal-rationalist spirit. The basis of the township appears to be utilitarian. Civic obligation exists because the citizen sees utility in it. He can calculate, that is, the gains to be acquired by participating in a politically efficacious organization. Thus, his membership has a prudential, self-interested basis which seems to characterize political life in the American village.

Other passages, though, indicate that Tocqueville emphasized a quite different facet of town politics. For Tocqueville, "the village is the only association which is so perfectly natural that, wherever a number of men are collected, it seems to constitute itself."[6] An association that is natural, that constitutes itself, cannot at the same time be the creation of rational, calculating men. The social bond must rather be of a more enduring, a more natural, substance. Indeed, Tocqueville found that New England communities are old and permanent, that "they have the support of the laws and the still stronger support of the manners of the community."⁷ The township is a traditional association: "The political education of the people has long been complete; say rather that it was complete when the people first set foot upon the soil."⁸ It is generally a polity of two or three thousand people, large enough to ensure that capable leaders can be found, yet small enough to permit an intimate, personalized form of social organization.⁹ Moreover, the township enables individuals to treat their neighbors not as means to an end, not as tools to be dealt with impersonally, but rather as ends in themselves to be regarded in the fullness of their humanity. In short, Tocqueville finds the existence of town spirit in America, a sense of community that makes the locality a vital democratic unit and, hence, a bulwark against the centralizing tendencies inherent in modern societies.¹⁰

This is an important and very attractive perspective. It appeals to our sense of justice, our desire for dignity, our yearning for freedom and social harmony. What is surprising, therefore, is the evident decline of communalist ideas in America throughout the many years between the Civil War and the Second World War. With few exceptions one is hard pressed to find systematic expression of the virtues of community democracy. Indeed, reformers such as George and Wilson, utopists such as Bellamy, elitists such as Henry Adams, even Social Darwinists such as Sumner—all virtually ignored the communalist tradition in favor of some kind of nationalist perspective. The precise reasons for this were complex. Westward expansion, industrialization, the development of a truly national communication system, growing involvement in world affairs—such factors may well have contributed in various ways to the demise of communalism. In any event, what is clear is that such a decline did in fact occur.

As regards local politics *per se*, the most important intellectual developments of the nineteenth century occurred in the judicial system and symbolized, I believe, precisely this decline in communalist thinking. I refer especially to what is sometimes termed the Cooley-Dillon controversy.

Thomas Cooley, an eminent judge and legal theorist of the nineteenth century, asserted the doctrine that local governments in the Anglo-Saxon world have an implicit but inviolable right to self-government. Anwar Syed, in his fine study of the history of ideas of American local government, summarizes the doctrine as follows:

> This right is inherent, in that it is ancient, and ought to rank with the other inviolable rights of Anglo-Saxon people.... One may go as far back as the Magna Charta and find that one of the guarantees that the barons at Runnymede wrested from King John related to the "ancient liberties and free customs" of London and all other cities.[11]

It is certainly true that the United States Constitution makes no mention of local government, and therefore confers no explicit rights on municipal corporations and other localities. However, as Syed notes, Cooley argued that

> a written constitution is never wholly expressive of the fundamental law of a state. It must be interpreted with reference to a people's settled convictions. To these the written word is subordinate. A constitution does not create but merely acknowledges or records the established rights of individuals and institutions. That certain rights have not been so recorded does not mean that they have been abolished.[12]

In supporting this position, Cooley relied heavily on Tocqueville's work. Like Tocqueville, he praised the American tradition of local self-government. He noted the long and honored history of this tradition in the United States, and agreed that the local community is the cradle and the guardian of democracy.[13] As such, its rights ought to be recognized and preserved.

This is an interesting and plausible argument. Its purely legal merits aside, it is in principle an argument for community government and local autonomy. It is also, however, an argument which has been consistently and decisively repudiated by the American judicial system. In 1868, John Dillon, chief justice of the Iowa Supreme Court, articulated what has come to be known as the Dillon Rule. According to Dillon, local governments are merely creatures of the state governments and, as such, can be created and destroyed at will. They have no residue of sovereignty, no inherent rights, no claim to special recognition or protection. Of course, Dillon's decision was rendered largely with reference to considerations of Constitutional law. But in its substance, and in the degree to which it has become a firmly entrenched doctrine, the Dillon Rule symbolized the fate of community democracy in America. Dillon articulated an essentially centralizing position which denied the existence of an implicit right of local self-government and which thus helped pave the way for a more managerial style of politics. By denying any privileged legal status to the local community, and by omitting any systematic reference to its supposed virtues, the Dillon Rule represents a significant rejection of the communalist perspective.

And again, the history of America in the late nineteenth and early twentieth centuries is largely devoid of serious communalist theory or practice. The great social and political movements of this time—the growth of capitalism, the rise of the political machine, Progressivism, and ultimately the New Deal—all either ignored or were inimical to the notion of community democracy. There were, to be sure, exceptions. Politically, the populist movement was based at least in part on principles of grassroots democracy similar to those of communalism. The so-called settlement-house movement and the community center movement in the early part of this century also relied on notions of community involvement and decision-making.[14] Intellectually, the political writings of John Dewey among others did present a clear and systematic statement of the communalist thesis, and will be mentioned again later in this chapter. But populism was, after all, a very short-lived movement, hardly a factor after 1896; and Dewey became influential not as a communalist but, rather, as a pluralist, a pragmatist, and something of a progressive.

It was not until the 1960s that a community orientation began to reassert itself on the American scene. Again, the Ford Foundation's Gray Areas Projects were crucial in this regard. But these projects were themselves contemporaneous and indeed bound up with the so-called President's Committee on Juvenile Delinquency and Crime, established by the Kennedy administration in 1961. This committee, though differing in crucial respects from the Ford Foundation, also adopted a community action perspective and funded similar kinds of community projects. By 1964, experimental community action programs existed in some twenty cities nationwide, with total support from Ford and government sources amounting to many millions of dollars. This experimentation bore fruit in 1965 with the War on Poverty and the Community Action Program to which roughly half of the Office of Economic Opportunity's budget was devoted. By 1969, more than one thousand Community Action Agencies were in existence, and while many of these were quite narrow in focus, many others engaged in a wide variety of activities, from child care and Head Start to job training and even political protest.[15]

The end of the Community Action Program has not signaled the end of community action in urban America. Indeed, some would argue that the neighborhood movement is stronger now than ever. In his study of neighborhood democracy, Yates lists nine different types of neighborhood or decentralized decisionmaking structures, all of which involve to one degree or another a communalist perspective. These include self-help organizations (neighborhood associations, tenants councils, etc.), community-based representatives of centralized agencies (little city halls, neighborhood ombudsmen), specialized service-delivery systems (neighborhood health centers and community school boards), and more complete structures of community control (community corporations).[16] These types of institutions are of course quite different from one another; their nature and function also vary considerably from city to city. Nonetheless, their very existence suggests that the neighborhood movement, and through it the communalist ideology, have become pervasive elements of the urban political scene, altering the decisionmaking process and presenting new options for dealing with urban problems.

These developments have sparked a renewed interest in communalism among scholars and intellectuals. Since the mid-1960s numerous books and articles on city politics have argued for a communalist approach to the urban crisis. While a comprehensive survey is not possible here, a few of the more influential texts merit special attention.

In some ways the earliest and most important statement was *Black Power* published by Stokely Carmichael and Charles Hamilton in 1967.[17] Though obviously concerned with questions that far transcend the city, Carmichael and Hamilton advocate neighborhood community control as a central mechanism of black power. In their view, neighborhood residents "should seek as their goal the actual control of the public schools in their community: hiring and firing of teachers, selection of teaching materials, determination of standards, etc."[18] Further, "tenants in buildings should form cohesive organizations—unions—to act in their common interest vis-à-vis the absentee slumlord."[19] Indeed, Carmichael and Hamilton propose a "community rebate plan," forcing merchants to reinvest forty to fifty percent of profits in the indigenous community.[20] More generally, the authors propose "a drive to revamp completely the present institutions of government," replacing older forms with new structures based on the principle of community control.[21] Of course, a central assumption of their work is the political and sociological primacy of race; their focus is explicitly and, in general, exclusively on black neighborhoods. Underlying this, though, is a distinctly communalist perspective emphasizing the value of participatory politics within geographically defined urban neighborhoods.

In 1969, Milton Kotler's *Neighborhood Government* was published and soon became perhaps the standard communalist work on the urban crisis.[22] A slim book in many ways, *Neighborhood Government* nonetheless does make a forceful and impassioned case for community control. Ignoring in large part the issue of race, Kotler adopts a vaguely leftist view, holding that the history of urban America is a history of neighborhoods being annexed and exploited by "a central neighborhood," thereby creating an "Imperial City." In each city, "Downtown" rules the rest of town, extracting—with the help of state governments—taxes and other forms of support for its own needs and interests. For Kotler, this is a perversion; in his view, urban neighborhoods are *political* rather than simply social or economic entities which, as such, should be self-governing. Indeed, the neighborhood is "the natural place for either founding new liberty or liberating local settlements from outside power."²³ This is so because the defining characteristic of the neighborhood is its "capacity for deliberative democracy."²⁴ Of course, the notion that the neighborhood is primarily a *political* entity is historically controversial. It is, nonetheless, a basic expression of communalist principles which Kotler uses to defend a "true radicalism" that has as its central aim the "gaining and preserving of local and democratic control."²⁵

A more conventional, liberal defense of the communalist view is to be found in Alan Altshuler's *Community Control*, published in 1970.²⁶ Still the most thorough and systematic analysis of practical political issues involved in community control, Altshuler's approach is essentially a pragmatic one. His defense of community control is based simply upon the need to equalize, at least to some degree, the game of American politics. Emphasizing, like Carmichael and Hamilton, the racial factor, Altshuler argues that the political powerlessness of American blacks must be redressed and that community control is a feasible method for doing so. Mindful of the many arguments against communalism, Altshuler nonetheless finds in the neighborhood movement an opportunity to revive urban democracy, increase participation among the disadvantaged and, at the same time, enhance the perceived legitimacy of the American political system.

With the publication of Charles Hampden-Turner's *From Poverty to Dignity*, community control received its most elaborate philosophic defense.²⁷ This book will be treated in more depth below. But in brief, Hampden-Turner argues for the psychosocial view that human dignity depends upon self-rule (i.e., a capacity to control one's own life), that the urban poor currently lack this capacity, and that therefore significant institutional reforms are needed so as to empower the poor. Hampden-Turner argues strongly in defense of Community Development Corporations, "permanent local institutions, owned and controlled by the local community, in and through which the local community decides and determines its own destiny."²⁸ A CDC dignifies the individuals who are part of it, offering them a sense of identity and purpose, providing them with an opportunity to wield political power, and ultimately teaching them the "art of democracy at the grassroots level."²⁹

Hampden-Turner's is a radical defense of communalism, based on an explicit theory of human development and calling for deep, nonincremental changes in the decisionmaking process.

The communalist ideology has thus been articulated in various ways and from a variety of perspectives. It is, in effect, a collection of related approaches to the urban crisis. These approaches, from Carmichael and Hamilton's emphasis on race to Hampden-Turner's focus on human development, are different in crucial ways. But they all share certain salient characteristics. Specifically, they all focus on a geographically defined entity, the urban neighborhood, and locate in that entity the seeds of democracy and political revival. Perhaps as importantly, they all identify and take their stand against a common enemy, namely, managerialism. Whether described as white power, as bourgeois reform, or as functionalist social science, the managerial mood is seen as the source of our inability to deal with urban problems, and as the basis of alienation and exploitation in American society.

CONVENTIONAL CRITIQUES

The rise of a communalist approach to urban problems in the past two decades has generated a great deal of controversy. By directly challenging the received wisdom, communalists have naturally made quite a few enemies. As a result, communalism itself has come in for much criticism from a variety of sources, criticism which has engendered, in turn, a heated debate.

Before reviewing the conventional critiques, however, two further distinctions within the communalist camp must be made. The first of these concerns the difference between administrative decentralization and true community control.[30] In brief, decentralization simply refers to the structural reorganization of existing public institutions so as to better serve the local community. A typical example would be the so-called little city hall, an experiment tried in several cities whereby the administration of certain policies is brought down to the grassroots level.[31] Such little city halls were designed to bring government closer to the people, but were not intended to transfer power to them. In contrast, genuine community control refers precisely to this kind of change, i.e., the devolution of full-scale political control over at least some policy areas to new and thoroughly indigenous institutions organized on a neighborhood basis. Typical here would be the Community Development Corporations mentioned above. Of course, there is between these extremes a rather large middle ground. As Altshuler notes in a somewhat different context, "community control should be conceived as a continuum rather than an absolute."[32] Nonetheless, the distinction between decentralization and community control is a crucial one. For while the entire range of approaches from decentralization to community control is inspired by communalist ideas, it is only toward the community control end that those ideas are truly embodied. And further, it is precisely with that end of the continuum that the critics of communalism have been most concerned.

A second distinction concerns the fact that the communalist ideology has been articulated both from the left and the right, thereby transcending the usual ideological divisions. Most of the authors mentioned above would be conventionally placed on the left of the political spectrum and indeed some, like Hampden-Turner, would be self-defined radicals. However, certain communalist principles have also been adopted by distinctly conservative thinkers. Robert Nisbet stands out as a prime example.[33] What distinguishes the more conservative variant is its veneration of community traditions and its willingness to tolerate and even encourage hierarchical or class-based forms of political organization internal to the community. Whereas the left vision sees community action as a liberating process in which neighborhood members can participate on an equal footing to develop fresh solutions to old problems, the conservative vision sees it as a process of rediscovery in which traditional approaches and ties are uncovered and nurtured under the leadership of a steward class. Communalists on the left envision a cooperative polity based on equal participation in public affairs; those on the right see a structured polity based on affective bonds, roughly reminiscent of the feudal commune. This is, without doubt, a crucial distinction which has its roots in the eighteenth- and nineteenth-century philosophic origins of communalism itself.

Nonetheless, despite this difference, all communalists share certain basic positions, including an emphasis on the urban neighborhood, on the feelings of community attachment to be developed therein, and on the need for a true sense of civic virtue or public-spiritedness which can counteract the atomism and egoism of modern bourgeois society.

Against this general perspective, three broad criticisms have been raised. According to the first, community control would further fragment the social fiber of urban America, solidifying the separation of the races, intensifying social discord, and undermining efforts to create a truly integrated and harmonious society.[34] Community control would pit neighborhood against neighborhood—black versus white, poor versus rich—in the scramble for scarce resources. The allegiance of urban residents would turn inward, toward the neighborhood community itself and away from the broad community of which we are all a part. Citywide goals would be sacrificed in the interests of a new parochialism featuring sharp in-group/out-group differences and conducive to mutual distrust and intolerance. As a result of all this, American urban society, which has been moving slowly toward healing its own wounds, would be torn apart once more, becoming a battleground for newly awakened racial and class-based animosities. The argument has been made perhaps most strongly by Irving Kristol in a famous article entitled "Decentralization for What?"[35]

A second criticism, somewhat related to the first, has been made by managerialists, largely as a response to the communalist attack on the managerial mood. In brief, according to managerialists community control would undermine the prospects for sound, rational planning in the city. By splitting up the power of decisionmaking into so many neighborhood units, the possibility of a unified and systematic approach to urban problems would essentially be destroyed. By vesting that power in the hands of grassroots organizations largely run by political amateurs, the opportunity for effective and professional leadership would be lost. By defining urban problems at the community or neighborhood level, the real, overarching problems that affect all neighborhoods would be overlooked, ignored, or dismissed as unmanageable. In general, then, managerialists see crucial goals such as rational central planning being sacrificed in pursuit of an ill-considered and ultimately unworkable participatory ideal.[36]

The third criticism, based more on empirical observations, argues that community control simply cannot work in practice. It argues that the key goal of widespread participation will just not be achieved through a community control strategy. A good deal of research has been undertaken examining the actual functioning of communalist experiments and, indeed, the results have not been encouraging. Scholars have discovered that rates of participation remain quite low, that levels of involvement tend to be higher in middle-class than in lower-class areas, that feelings of community attachment and political efficacy are not dramatically improved, and that the so-called iron law of oligarchy holds as well for community organizations as for other kinds of organizations.[37] Such scholars conclude that simply conferring power to the neighborhoods will not, in and of itself, produce the participatory ideal so strongly cherished by communalists.

These are weighty criticisms which have presented considerable practical problems for the advocates of communalism. In purely theoretical terms, however, I would contend that they leave communalism virtually unaffected. Indeed, the communalist has simple responses to these criticisms which are, in my view, nearly unassailable.

To begin with, existing empirical evidence does not unambiguously support the three critiques. Indeed, there is little or no data to suggest that community control would exacerbate social conflict or that it would undermine the pursuit of citywide goals; and while there is, again, evidence to suggest that community control does not increase levels of political participation, this evidence can hardly be considered final or definitive. Moreover, there is absolutely no reason to believe that the three criticisms are self-evidently true. For example, the notion that community control would produce social conflict is by no means obvious. Perhaps conferring genuine decisionmaking power over key policy areas would *reduce* conflict, making neighborhood residents less defensive, less frustrated, and more interested in working to achieve tangible, practicable results.

But more important, the conventional critiques largely ignore the value premises and underlying philosophic assumptions implicit in the communalist perspective. To argue that community control will produce social conflict is to ignore the possibility that certain forms of social conflict may in some circumstances be extremely desirable. To contend that community control will undermine efforts at integration is, again, to presume that integration is the highest priority. To lament the alleged loss of efficiency, economy, and professionalism is to deny without argument that these things, valuable as they may be, might also be worth sacrificing in the interest of other, more sublime values.

The communalist ideology, like managerialism, is based upon a number of underlying philosophic positions concerning the nature of man, moral judgment, political obligation, and the public realm. If we are to truly understand and intellectually assess this perspective, then we must uncover and consider in some detail its intellectual foundations.

COMMUNALISM AND THE THEORISTS OF ALIENATION

At the philosophic core of the communalist ideology lies the concept of alienation. Overworked, hackneyed, twisted beyond its original meaning, alienation nonetheless remains a powerful idea in modern social thought. Among other things, it is—like communalism itself—a notion that transcends traditional ideological boundaries. Perhaps most often associated with existential philosophy, as in Sartre's notion of "bad faith," alienation is also a staple of contemporary nostalgic conservatism, of nineteenth- and twentieth-century positivist sociology, of Marxist humanism, of the new left, and so on. Writers as diverse as Hegel and Marx, Durkheim and Lukács, Herbert Marcuse and Robert Nisbet may all be considered theorists of alienation.

Two things unite these very different writers. First, each has a concept of human nature, a normative and even metaphysical notion of what constitutes a whole, fully human person, a standard from which actual people—for a variety of reasons—have strayed. Man, in other words, has become separated or estranged from his better nature; and this constitutes in large part the condition we call alienation. Second, each of these writers, both of the left and of the right, finds the sources of alienation to lie in the cultural system of liberal/bourgeois society, of which one important offshoot is the managerial mood. The philosophy of the Enlightenment in particular is seen to have led to the alienation of the human spirit from its intellectual, social, and political moorings.

According to the communalist view, the world in which we live is in some sense indeterminate. It presents us with a number of possibilities, but forces none of these possibilities upon us. We are, in effect, adrift in a currentless sea and as a result must rely on our own initiative, judgment, and genius in order to create a life for ourselves. Stated negatively, this is a view which denies the guidance of God, or of natural law, or of some other metaphysical principle but which denies, equally, the causal, machinelike, stimulus-response image of the world, an image associated with the Enlightenment philosophers and their heirs. In short, it rejects all forms of reductionism in the explication of human behavior and therefore sees the world as an inexplicable, almost mysterious realm of nearly limitless variety and potential. Stated positively, this is a view which celebrates above all human freedom, not merely freedom from external constraint but the freedom to create—virtually from nothing or, rather, from the nearly infinite but indeterminate materials presented to us—a life, an identity, indeed an essence.[38] In short, it is a humanistic perspective in that it sees man as a fundamentally self-created being. We construct the world, we make ourselves what we are, we are responsible for the nature and quality of human existence. And it is in this power that our freedom and very dignity as human beings lie.[39]

As regards social or political matters, it must be added that individuals create themselves only in concert with others. That is, while individuals act as individuals, they do so only with other individuals. As Dewey writes:

> Wants, choices and purposes have their locus in single beings; behavior which manifests desires, intent and resolution proceeds from them in their singularity. But only intellectual laziness leads us to conclude that since the form of thought and

decision is individual, their content, their subject-matter, is also something purely personal.... Singular things act, but they act together. Nothing has been discovered which acts in entire isolation.... There is no mystery about the fact of association, of an interconnected action which affects the activity of singular elements. There is no sense in asking how individuals come to be associated. They exist and operate in association.[40]

Thus, the self-creativity of the human spirit is, at least in some sense, a social process, a collaborative effort dependent upon structures of communication, cooperation, and empathy.

To be alienated, then, is to be separated from this process of self-determination. More specifically, it is, first, to be denied the feeling of self-mastery and to be subjected to the real or imagined domination of something external, be it another person, an institution, one's own baser instincts, perhaps even an idea. Second, to be aliented is to be taken out of the collaborative, interactive process of mutual self-determination and forced to act as a discrete, isolated, and relatively helpless atom. Again, the historical sources of such alienation are to be found in the philosophy of the Enlightenment and in its related institutions. By regarding man as at base a sensuous creature, a higher-order animal seeking to maximize pleasure and minimize pain, the Enlightenment robbed man of his dignity and his capacity for freedom, rendering him a slave to his passions. By seeing government as little more than a means to achieving material ends, i.e., physical comfort, the Enlightenment undermined the notion of community, substituting a preordained set of goals for the collaborative, deliberative process envisioned by the theorists of alienation. And by understanding freedom solely in a formal sense as the absence of arbitrary political constraint, the Enlightenment denied the broader sense of freedom as the basis of human dignity and worth, indeed as an end in itself.

It is not surprising, then, that the first great critic of the Enlightenment was also the first, and perhaps greatest exponent of the communalist ideology. I refer, of course, to Rousseau.[41] Rousseau's attack on the idea of progress was discussed in the previous chapter. But his critique of the Enlightenment went far beyond that, and it is to this broader critique that we now turn.

It must be emphasized at the outset that Rousseau's political thought is exceedingly complex and at times seemingly inconsistent. This accounts, in part, for the diverse interpretations his writings have prompted. For some he was a great apostle of radical individualism, for others a holist and organicist; according to one view he was the great source of "democratic totalitarianism," whereas for another he was, at base, a conservative and a reactionary. Indeed, Rousseau himself was at pains to proclaim the consistency of his work, thereby acknowledging at least tacitly its seemingly contradictory character.

These strands do converge, however, if we see Rousseau as a communalist, indeed as the source of communalism in all of its various incarnations. One strand is, to be sure, an individualist strand. We see evidence of this in the early parts of Rousseau's "Discourse on the Origin of Inequality," in the *Emile*, and perhaps in certain of his autobiographical writings, especially the *Reveries of the Solitary Walker*. In these various works, one finds a kind of early humanistic picture of man. For Rousseau, the defining characteristic of human nature is its very malleability. Depending upon circumstance, men can be idle and aimless creatures, driven only by physical want and desire, and possessing nothing but an inarticulate, inchoate sense of sympathy for the suffering; or they can be prideful and deceitful manipulators of society, dissemblers in search of wealth and power and prestige; or they can be confident and self-determined participants in a "general will" that seeks to promote in a rational and enlightened manner the interests of society as a whole. While Rousseau is clear that factors beyond our control influence what we become, he also seems to suggest that we have some real choices to make, that as individuals we can, for example, choose to embrace or renounce the freedom and self-mastery that is ultimately the basis of human dignity and worth.

Rousseau is, thus, something of an individualist in the humanistic tradition. And yet, there is a second, clearly communalist strand which is equally characteristic of his thought. We can discover this, for example, in the Dedication to Geneva of the "Discourse on the Origin of Inequality," and also in such political writings as *The Government of Poland* and the

Letter to D'Alembert. In each of these writings, Rousseau emphasizes the political or social importance of solidarity—of harmony, conformity, and unity—even at the expense of individualism. For political reasons, that is, the freedom and power of the individual may have to be curbed, his better nature made alien, in order that the goals of society be achieved.

The resolution of the rather clear tension between these strands is to be found in the first half of Rousseau's magisterial work on the *Social Contract*.[42] While a satisfactory account of this resolution cannot be attempted here, some of its more salient features can be outlined.

The very purpose of the *Social Contract* is to justify certain principles which properly resolve the contrary tendencies of individual and society. But what must be emphasized is that, for Rousseau, a proper resolution would do violence neither to the ends of the body politic nor to the dignity and autonomy— the *individuality*—of the individual. In other words, he felt that *both* sets of claims, personal and political, are valid and necessary, and that neither is justly compromised. Thus, his self-appointed task was to reconcile two powerful and seemingly opposed tendencies—one promoting particularity, the other solidarity—without giving in to either.

This project can be looked at in a variety of ways. In conceptual terms, it involved the identification of a series of political principles that would resurrect the notion of a true public interest—a genuine and uncontaminated sense of communal purpose and civic virtue—without qualifying or subsuming the independence of the individual. In historical terms, it involved the reconciliation of classical political ideals, in which the claims of the community are the only really valid claims, with the modern ideal, in which individual rights alone are natural and sacred. In this sense, the classical vision would have to be rejected because it ignores the requirements of the individual, particularly the requirement of autonomy upon which Rousseau based man's moral faculty. But the modern view is equally inadequate, at least in part because it rests on a bogus, contrived notion of the public interest.

Rousseau's solution takes the form of the general will. While this conception is difficult and often baffling, we are fortunate in that a few of its more unambiguous aspects are especially pertinent to the subject at hand. Specifically, when fully operative Rousseau's general will amounts to the absolute exclusion of particularity from the realm of politics. The general will considers only general questions. And it promulgates laws in a strictly "disinterested" fashion, laws that apply to all equally, without reference to particular considerations. Its criteria are rigorously universalistic. Only principles of justice and right are considered, principles aimed solely at securing the common good. With such a conception, Rousseau seeks to reestablish the grounds for something analogous to classical civic virtue. Selfishness and egoism are bracketed out or neutralized. The good of the community is the only legitimate political consideration.

But equally important, the general will also involves the full development of the individual as an autonomous rational being. Coincident with, and basic to, the general will is the moral perfection of the individual. Rousseau's "citizen" is an enlightened individual who acts in terms of justice, right, and duty. His orientation is general and public-spirited. His devotion to the polity is complete. And yet, he retains—in altered and improved form—his personal liberty and his independence. Indeed, moral perfection—which is politically necessary—implies and requires this independence. The citizen of the well-constructed state obeys only himself. He conquers his selfish inclinations, overcomes the tyranny of others, and thereby becomes his own master.

Now these well-known principles are complex and quite controversial. Again, this is not the place to discuss their genesis or their coherence. But I do want to emphasize the following: Rousseau sought to elucidate principles which involve the complete *interpenetration* of the social and the individual without subsuming either one to the other. The individual's freedom, his self-mastery, and his autonomy are not merely incidental to the establishment of civic order; they are, in fact, necessary conditions of that order. Civic virtue, according to Rousseau, is such only if based on free and voluntary choice. An imposed or manufactured sense of loyalty would fail to resolve the individual-social problem. It would ignore the autonomy of the individual; at the same time, it would provide at best an unreliable foundation for politics. Thus, in the system of the *Social Contract* a healthy body politic requires citizens whose allegiance is not only complete but also freely, rationally, and self-consciously given. Indeed, as Rousseau said, the individual "*has* a general will" only by virtue of his moral liberty.

It is clear that, with this formulation, the needs of the body politic are satisfied. Citizens are entirely committed to the well-being of the community. All of those things that threaten civic order—particularity and prejudice, pride and faction—are neutralized or eliminated. Rights are replaced by duties. But, at the same time, the requirements of the individual are also met. Civic virtue and devotion to the community must be based on moral liberty. The individual's freedom and dignity are thus enhanced and preserved. Only in this circumstance can there be a truly satisfactory and enduring solution to the individual-social problem in which, as Rousseau implies, the will of all and the general will are one and identical. Thus, in the argument of the *Social Contract*, citizenship involves a freely chosen sense of loyalty and obligation. That this choice is rational and voluntary means that it is a moral and personally dignifying act; that it involves a deep-seated sense of community means that the political order can flourish.

For Rousseau, then, the solution to alienation is to be found in the participatory community. By becoming involved in an authentic communal process aimed at identifying and pursuing the common good, the individual solves two problems. First, he embraces his true nature, realizing his potential as a self-determined and genuinely free individual. And second, he enters into a bond of brotherhood with his fellow citizens, thereby overcoming the unnatural separation of individuals so characteristic of the bourgeois world. To the degree that the first is emphasized but not the second, we have a solution perhaps more congenial to communalists of the left than of the right; to the degree that the second is given priority, we have a more conservative approach. Rousseau's work is striking in that it embraces both sides of the question and, indeed, demonstrates their compatibility and, more, their mutual dependence. Communalism implies that individuals gain control over their lives, and do so precisely by joining with other individuals in a common, morally uplifting pursuit of the public interest.[43]

The impact of these Rousseauian notions on the subsequent history of political thought is open to much dispute. For purposes of the present argument, however, we can stipulate certain general lines of influence. Thus, for example, the ideas of Rousseau the communitarian—who so lavishly praised his father, that simple, hard-working, and deeply patriotic citizen of Geneva—can be found reflected in the writings of certain conservatives of the counterrevolutionary period in post-Napoleonic France, especially Joseph deMaistre; in the theoretical treatises of certain of the classical sociologists, notably Emile Durkheim; and finally, in those writers of the twentieth century obsessed with the problem of "mass society" such as Robert Nisbet. But Rousseau the humanist and individualist—the architect of Emile's education, for example—can also be discerned in the Romantic tradition, with its celebration of individual engagement and self-definition, as well as in Romanticism's various Nietzschean, Bergsonian, and existentialist offshoots. Few writers, however, have captured and reflected the *dual* emphasis on community and individual self-mastery, the notion that individualist/humanist goals can be best achieved through participation in an authentically constituted, communally-based polity. Exceptions to this would be, perhaps, certain writers in the anarchist tradition, notably Proudhon and Sorel. Indeed, both Proudhon and Sorel were political radicals who were, at the same time, moral conservatives, emphasizing the sanctity of traditional family life and advocating a type of cooperative communal existence based upon the individual's freely chosen sense of oneness with his neighbors or fellow workers. As such, of course, both Proudhon and Sorel were, in their different ways, reflecting a general line of thought most forcefully articulated by the young Karl Marx. Indeed, Marx's early essay on "Alienated Labor" in the so-called *Paris Manuscripts* remains a standard source of alienation theory. To be sure, his analysis emphasizes the economic or material, rather than cultural, sources of alienation; the individual is alienated largely because the product of his labor has been taken away from him.[44] But

Marx's description of the dimensions of alienation rings a familiar bell; the individual is alienated both from his self, his "species-being," and also from the community, his fellow laborers.⁴⁵ And further, Marx's image of a nonalienated world also fits our general picture well; it is the kind of society in which individuals, by identifying with and nurturing the interest of the community as a whole, thereby ennoble themselves and attain that degree of emancipation that is the true source of human dignity and self-respect.⁴⁶

I believe this general kind of argument constitutes the philosophic underpinning of the communalist approach to contemporary urban problems. As may be expected, one rarely finds pointed or systematic reference to the twofold nature of alienation or to the twofold solution to that problem. But contemporary communalism is, in my view, based on the notion that the modern managerialist city is a fundamental source of alienation, that this alienation essentially involves the unsatisfying and even traumatic separation of the individual from his true self and from his neighbors, and that the overcoming of this separation can best be achieved through a process of community problem solving or neighborhood democracy.

The clearest articulation of these notions among contemporary communalists is to be found in Hampden-Turner's *From Poverty to Dignity*. Hampden-Turner's defense of Community Development Corporations is itself based on an explicit theory of human development and human liberation. According to this theory, individuals become truly human only if they are able to enjoy a genuinely free existence. Such an existence, moreover, essentially involves the power of individuals to define, and thereby create, an identity for themselves. This is a power too often denied the poor in America's cities:

> There is great *definitional power* as well as creativity in the right to label reality and have that label stick. "The Negro problem," "right to work laws," "ghetto violence," "separatist thinking," "culture of poverty," "extremism," "socialized medicine," are all examples of opprobrious labeling which has helped to stall much-needed responses to the plight of the poor.⁴⁷

Liberation involves the capacity to perceive reality from one's own viewpoint, to define that reality in terms of that viewpoint, and to attain thereby a sense of identity and competence. To be denied such liberation is to be alienated from one's true nature. Indeed, according to Hampden-Turner,

> What is required for psycho-social development is the broadest possible synthesis of competences, including political, economic, moral, persuasive, benefactory, physical, technical and organizational *competence*. [A]ll these kinds of *competence must be integrated and fused* if poor people are to develop.[48]

The result of human liberation is the experience of self-confirmation or self-actualization which constitutes, in effect, the negation of self-alienation. Most importantly, the method of achieving this negation, and the test by which we determine the degree to which it has been achieved, involves the individual's active participation in the affairs of the world.

> To act in real life situations so as to experience the consequences is fundamental to psycho-social learning. There can be no liberation without *demonstration*, literally "showing what you mean."

Stated otherwise, it is by exercising one's faculties to the fullest, by accepting the risks entailed in commitment and participation, that one overcomes the alienation inherent in the modern bourgeois culture of American cities.

Hampden-Turner's perspective relies upon a particular vocabulary of psychosocial development, one which is not generally used by theorists of politics and the value of which will here be left unexplored. But clearly, we can see in Hampden-Turner's work the communalists' more general emphasis on self-mastery, on collective and cooperative endeavor, and on the liberating effects of political involvement. Virtually all defenses of urban community control are based, explicitly or implicitly, on themes such as these. Thus, for example, Carmichael and Hamilton contend that "Black people must redefine themselves, and only *they* can do that"; they favor "broadening the base of political participation"; and they call for "Black people in this country to unite, to recognize their heritage, to build a sense of community" and to "define their own goals, to lead their organizations and to support those organizations."⁵⁰ For Milton Kotler, both liberty and territoriality are "natural" to man; the modern city, which undermines liberty and destroys territorial control, thereby separates man from his natural impulses.⁵¹ According to Morris and Hess, "when people, or at least many people, in a neighborhood finally decide that they want to participate in politics and not just delegate power to politicians, then community politics begins, local liberty becomes a possibility, and the debates over neighborhood government sensibly begin."⁵² All of these perspectives see contemporary municipal government, with its decidedly managerialist orientation, as depriving individuals of the materials to become full and free citizens controlling their lives and fulfilling their potential in concert with one another. And all of them focus on neighborhood government, in one form or another, as the institutional means for correcting this most serious situation.

Again, Hampden-Turner's defense of neighborhood government as an institutional solution is the most systematic. As indicated above, his particular emphasis is on the so-called Community Development Corporation. He regards the CDC as a truly radical answer to the problems of the urban poor in that it confers real power to neighborhoods. Specifically, in a CDC residents do not merely participate in the decisionmaking process. Rather, they "participate in *creating the opportunity structure itself,* and hence gain some control over the social reality of their neighborhoods."⁵³ That is, a CDC is viewed as a genuine republic-in-miniature in which the members control the structure, resources, procedures, and plans. As such, it is a source of both community and liberty, creating "a new solidarity" and "symbols of community respect"⁵⁴ and providing a context in which individuals can be taught "the arts of democracy at the grass-roots level."⁵⁵

It should be noted that Hampden-Turner specifically rejects the example of the War on Poverty's Community Action Agencies as structures imposed from without by "absentee thinkers." In his view, institutional solutions will work only if they are indigenously designed and generated. Nonetheless, his general perspective on neighborhood government, emphasizing as it does the liberation of the individual and the strengthening of community ties, is characteristic of communalists as a group, regardless of the particular institutional mechanism each happens to advocate. Thus, for example, Kotler also focuses on the CDC, and devotes much attention to a case study of one such corporation in Columbus, Ohio. Writers such as Altshuler, Morris and Hess, and even Carmichael and Hamilton are less specific as to their favored institutional solution. But in all cases, an *increased* level of community control is desirable because of its consequences for participation, solidarity, and the general problem of alienation. Indeed, it is precisely this kind of concern that distinguishes communalists from noncommunalist advocates of neighborhood government, for example, those who take a "political marketplace" approach as discussed in the next chapter.[56]

THE ETHICS OF COMMUNALISM

The philosophical arguments outlined above are widely praised for their recognition of human dignity and liberation. At the same time, however, and for many of the same reasons, they have serious and controversial consequences for ethical thinking in general. Indeed, while ostensibly based on a deeply felt ethical commitment to the dignity of the individual, the communalist view of man and of man's role in the world has been criticized, with some justification, for undermining moral thinking altogether, for inviting a brand of nihilism as complete and as dangerous as that sanctioned, at least implicitly, by managerialism.

The problem can be stated succinctly. According to the communalist view, humans are fulfilled only when they achieve self-mastery, when they control their lives, when they create their very life-structures. Included in these life-structures, of course, are political processes, economic relationships, social organizations, and cultural systems. But also included are principles of ethics. An individual is alienated when political decisions are imposed upon him, when the product of his labor is taken from him, when his self-image is provided for him by someone else; but he is equally alienated when notions of right and wrong are presented to him as givens, as facts about which he can do nothing. According to the philosophy of alienation, morality is—like the rest of our sociocultural world—a human creation. To renounce the capacity to formulate, not simply discover, ethical principles is to fall once again into the vicious circle of alienation.

This position has complex and difficult theoretical implications. To begin with, the ethics of communalism—for that is what we are treating—are based on a denial of "higher" moral truths. In particular, the two great sources of moral insight in the history of the West, natural law and the law of God, are rejected as being either unknowable or nonexistent. To believe in natural or divine law is to alienate our reason, to become a slave to some reified phantasm of our own making which, nonetheless, comes perversely to rule us. A further implication, then, is that all moral codes are, wittingly or otherwise, manmade. Our notions of right and wrong come to us through tradition or conscious decision; but they are, in all cases, the product of some kind of *human* process. They are, that is, artificial.

To this point, of course, there is fair agreement between managerialist and communalist ethics. Each rejects the notion of immutable moral truths and each has been, therefore, subject to the charge of nihilism, of being unable to offer a substantial and persuasive set of objectively true ethical principles. Where they part, however, is on the issue of human autonomy, and their differences in this regard are crucial.[57]

In brief, whereas managerialists generally adopt one or another form of utilitarianism, communalism as an ideology rejects utilitarianism as yet another source of alienation, i.e., as a subversion of human autonomy. Utilitarianism typically involves the maximization of some previously defined, philosophically underived good, e.g., "pleasure" or something else that we desire or have an inclination for. Like the higher-order animals that we are, we seek to gratify our needs, urges, and passions; and the degree to which a particular social policy permits the widespread gratification of such passions is the degree to which it is a morally acceptable policy. The communalist perspective, however, implicitly denies that we are merely higher-order animals. Animals do not suffer alienation because, indeed, they are incapable of self-mastery.

Humans alone create their own worlds and, thus, are alone in being able to act on the basis of self-generated principles rather than biologically given needs and desires. Indeed, to act in terms of inclination is to be controlled by something alien to the human spirit, namely, the human body, hence to renounce the possibility of human dignity. Moral man is autonomous man; but autonomy means, above all, freedom from the passions, from one's baser self.

This crucial, unstated premise—that freedom necessarily involves freedom from the body, from the passions, from mere inclination—is, in my judgment, basic to the communalist ideology. It is in Rousseau, the great source of communalism, that we again find the origins of this doctrine. In the *Social Contract* Rousseau writes as follows:

> The passage from the state of nature to the civil state produces a very remarkable change in man, by substituting justice for instinct in his conduct, and giving his actions the morality they had formerly lacked. Then only, when the voice of duty takes the place of physical impulses and right of appetite, does man, who so far had considered only himself, find that he is forced to act on different principles, and to consult his reason before listening to his inclinations. [T]he mere impulse of appetite is slavery, while obedience to a law which we prescribe to ourselves is liberty.[58]

This notion, extended by Kant and Hegel and adopted, more or less explicitly, by Rousseau's heirs on the left and the right, is implicit in all contemporary communalism. The communalist emphasis on alienation, on the twin problems of liberty and community, is precisely a turning away from considerations of mere utility and material prosperity, from the "petty and paltry pleasures" ridiculed by Tocqueville, in favor of a rather more elevated set of values. The provision of wealth, of material benefits, does not suffice; an animal that is well fed and comfortable remains, just the same, an animal. Humans require more. They require, again, a sense of self-rule—including a sense of moral autonomy—that far transcends the usual considerations of utilitarianism. To be not merely well fed but ennobled, to feel not merely pleasure but a sense of dignity and self-esteem—these are the underlying goals of communalism.

The implications for neighborhood government are crucial. For the institutions of community control are to be valued, therefore, not for the policies they will bring about, not for their potential contribution to the material well-being of the poor, not even for their implications for justice. Rather, they are to be valued as sources of liberty and activism, hence as sources of dignity and self-esteem. Indeed, neighborhood government is to be valued almost entirely for the spiritual benefits it will confer.

But what of the charge of nihilism? If moral autonomy is a necessary fact of life which needs only to be made manifest, are we then free to adopt any set of moral principles we wish? Can we decide right and wrong simply out of thin air, to suit our own purposes? Is anything justified? In effect, those who adopt a "noncognitivist" view of ethics—who regard ethical principles as being based ultimately on attitude and taste, hence as incapable of philosophic justification—would seem forced to answer yes. And their opponents, e.g., defenders of natural law, would seize upon this as, itself, proof of the nihilism and moral bankruptcy of the noncognitivist perspective.

In my judgment, the ethics of communalism are at least partly exempt from this charge for at least two reasons. To begin with, and as indicated above, not every moral standpoint is justified. Specifically, ethical judgments based primarily on desire or self-interest are to be ruled out altogether. One must distinguish right from wrong in terms of principle, not in terms of selfish motivation. And thus, not just any standpoint is morally acceptable. Whether this view is only of procedural importance, or whether it also has necessary substantive implications, is an old and extraordinarily difficult question. Hegel, for example, argued that Kant's principled ethics were purely formal, that they told one how to be moral but not what specific actions morality consisted of and that, as a result, *any* action could be morally justified in terms of Kant's categorical imperative. On an account such as this, then, one could argue that communalist ethics are potentially compatible with any political arrangement or decision. One cannot, however, argue that they are compatible with any set of motivations. Stated otherwise, anything can perhaps be justified, but it must be done for the right reasons. For many critics, this qualification would suffice to save communalism from the charge of moral nihilism.

Beyond this, and if taken to their logical conclusions, communalist ethics are compatible only with a democratic, indeed a radically democratic, decisionmaking process. This is the crucial political implication of communalism in general. For again, communalist ethics are based upon the notion that individuals ought to be their own masters. A citizen is truly free only if he can determine the particulars of his own existence. Politically, this implies that decisionmaking arrangements are morally acceptable only if they give each individual an opportunity to make significant political choices. Such a perspective presumably rules out all forms of traditional elite rule—from the so-called oriental despotism to modern constitutional monarchy—insofar as they require individuals to obey the instructions of someone else. It also seems to rule out all forms of "democratic elitism,"[59] including republican and representative forms of democracy, insofar as these require individuals to cede their decisionmaking powers to some other group or individual. Indeed, according to a few writers, virtually all standard forms of political association would be ruled out by the requirement of self-obedience.

The clearest contemporary statement of this latter view is to be found in Robert Paul Wolff's *In Defense of Anarchism*. Wolff's problem is essentially the same as Rousseau's: How can individuals join together in a political society ruled by law without, at the same time, sacrificing their right to rule themselves? That is, how can the citizen obey the law and still be obeying only himself? Of course, for Rousseau the solution lay in the notion of a general will—an entity or, more precisely, a process by which citizens come together to decide political questions solely in terms of the public interest, thereby authenticating their own moral worth. For Wolff, on the other hand, Rousseau's solution—and virtually all other solutions— will not work. According to Wolff, the individual has not merely a right but a duty to obey only himself; the moment he confers the right of decision to something or someone else—be it a legislature, the majority, even a "general will"—he thereby sacrifices his moral autonomy, a move which for Wolff can never be justified on ethical grounds. Thus, the notion of self-obedience or self-mastery is to be taken quite literally. There can be no law, no government, in the traditional sense.

Wolff, therefore, advocates "anarchism," by which is meant not chaos and "anarchy" but, rather, a form of political association based on cooperation rather than coercion. Conformity, unity, order, and collective action—indeed, all the requisites of political society—are to be achieved not through the coercive enforcement of law but rather through the cooperative agreements of free and rational individuals. We have, then, a picture of the political community as a harmonious cooperative entity; and this is a picture adopted, explicitly or implicitly, by virtually all exponents of communalism. I am arguing, in effect, that the political tendencies and perhaps even the logical implications of communalism are anarchist, that they involve an image of each particular community generating its own consensus—based upon shared needs and values, a shared tradition, mutual empathy and identity, and the like—a consensus in which each voice is heard and has a significant impact. It is true that various communalists talk of the role of leadership, of majority rule, even of representative assemblies of various kinds. But the underlying thrust and logic of the position—based as it is on a philosophy of human wholeness and self-mastery and on the maintenance of moral autonomy—looks toward a decision-making process involving cooperation and consensus rather than coercion and control.

Again, the degree to which the requirement of self-obedience is compatible with, say, representative or majoritarian forms of democracy is open to considerable dispute. Wolff's account may be mistaken.[60] But what is clear is that the communalist doctrine of political obligation must be based solely on the notion of self-obedience. For the communalist, all efforts at neighborhood government must not merely take into account but be ruled by the articulated judgments of the members. If alienation is to be annulled, if individuals are to be truly liberated, then neighborhood government must somehow reflect and affirm the principle of self-obedience. And in seeking this goal, the image of community as a cooperative rather than coercive entity remains at the heart of the communalist ideology.

If communalist ethics thereby imply a theory of political obligation, then they also imply a theory of the public realm. In brief, according to communalism, the purpose of political life is fundamentally spiritual. Its goal, in essence, is to produce good citizens who will be moved to engage in political life and do so primarily with the interests of the community at heart. Indeed, what we have here is a contemporary species of civic humanism which, as such, defines virtuous citizenship as the basis of human self-fulfillment in general.[61] Participation in the public life of the community or the urban neighborhood is seen as an end in itself, something inherently good regardless of its substantive consequences. And thus, again, the purpose of politics does not primarily involve the formulation of sound public policy or the attainment of peace and prosperity; nor does it essentially involve the just distribution of goods and services or the efficient production of wealth. The emphasis, rather, is on the political process itself. To be engaged with one's neighbors in an earnest and healthy search for the common good, to participate in an open deliberative process aimed at securing the public interest, is to overcome the alienation so characteristic of liberal bourgeois society. That is the primary goal of the communalist ideology.

4. POSSESSIVE-INDIVIDUALISM

The ideal communalist polity is a healthy and vigorous democracy. It pursues the good of the whole while at the same time protecting and enhancing the personal freedoms of its individual citizens. What does one do, however, with citizens who refuse to go along? What of the citizen, for example, who regards this open deliberative process as a sham, a delusion, even a waste of time? or the individual who participates fully in the communal decisionmaking process only to be dissatisfied with its results? or the person who cares not one whit for the "public interest," who steadfastly pursues his own interests without regard for the welfare of his neighbors? Such questions raise the issue of anarchy, not anarchism, and point to the general problem of "majority tyranny," of the community imposing its will on recalcitrant members. It is a thorny problem for communalists, but many simply ignore it, as though wishing it away. Indeed, among contemporary theorists of urban neighborhood democracy one can find little systematic effort to treat this problem. Historically, the case is rather different, but the answers provided by communalists of the past have been controversial, to say the least. Emblematic here is Rousseau's famous, intractable assertion that those who fail to go along must be "forced to be free," one of the most striking, bedeviling, and ultimately inflammatory justifications of political coercion ever attempted.

In the face of this problem, there are those who have asserted that it is simply insoluble, that communalist structures necessarily imply majority tyranny in one form or another, and that majority tyranny itself is no less noxious and oppressive than any other variety of tyranny. Such writers, in seeking political arrangements that would avoid this problem, have placed their emphasis on the rights and liberties of individuals *against* the community. On this account, communalist notions of the public interest and the common good are dangerous. The phrase "forced to be free" symbolizes the hopeless contradictions of the communalist ideology and the threat it poses to the well-being of the individual. Only by making individual rights and freedoms paramount, only by making them the bases of political order, can a healthy and truly humane public sector be established, one that is invulnerable to the more extreme and disquieting possibilities of political life.

By identifying so strongly with the rights of the individual, however, such critics of communalism are also critics of managerialism. For the managerialists, with their emphasis on efficiency and economy, on a scientifically managed quest for the common good, pose an equal or even greater threat to basic rights and liberties. Indeed, as was suggested in Chapter 2, even democracy itself may be sacrificed to the excesses of managerialism.

Those writers, then, who have cast their lot with the individual comprise yet a third group; they offer a distinctive ideology of urban politics which, like the others, relies on certain fundamental principles of political philosophy in dealing with the day-to-day problems of our cities. This ideology has been called "neoconservatism," though for reasons to be elaborated later on the label is both too inclusive and too restrictive. It is an ideology of individual rights, and it is, to be sure, often associated with certain elements of America's right wing.

Interestingly, recent purveyors of this ideology tend to have had liberal or even radical backgrounds. Some may have had flirtations with communist or socialist movements. Others may have been dyed-in-the-wool New Dealers, champions of big government and postwar liberalism. The changes that many of these individuals underwent can perhaps be attributed to a disillusionment with those broader movements, disillusionment with Soviet repression, for example, or with the bureaucratic legacy of the New Deal. In any event, the more proximate sources of disillusionment are clear. To begin with, the writers I have in mind react sharply against the "best and brightest" motif in American politics, the preoccupation with expertise and scientific training characteristic of the managerial mood. They embrace, that is to say, a general cynicism about the effectiveness of science, especially social science, in formulating public policy; and in so doing they actually echo the criticisms of communalists. However, they also react sharply against the counterculture motif in American politics, the preoccupation with humanism and populism characteristic of the communalist ideology. They embrace, that is to say, a general cynicism about the modern citizen himself and his capacity for self-government; and in so doing, they thereby adopt at least one significant aspect of the managerialist critique.

Thus, the writers I have in mind accept to a great extent the arguments of managerialism and communalism *against* one another while accepting none of the arguments each uses in its own behalf. And in this vacuum they have formulated—or, rather, rediscovered and refashioned—an ideology of possessive-individualism. This transcends conventional left-right distinctions. It embraces, consciously or otherwise, broad aspects of Anglo-American liberalism—more of the classic Lockeian variety than of the "republican" variety—and forges something of a synthesis aimed above all at avoiding the perils of tyranny. While important as a general political ideology, it has also been significant in shaping the controversy surrounding the urban crisis and urban public policy. Indeed, there is some evidence that possessive-individualism is actually the ascendant approach to urban problems, one especially compatible with emerging trends in American national politics.

The actual impact of possessive-individualism is hard to gauge. This may be because it is, in essence, a negative or critical ideology which, because of the historical contexts of its reemergence, seeks to debunk and dispel rather than create. We are hard pressed to find possessive-individualist "experiments" in urban government; possessive-individualists tend to be uncomfortable with experiments. There are no sweeping and eye-catching programs or policies of possessive-individualism aimed at solving the problems of our cities; possessive-individualists do not usually like such programs. Yet the impact of the possessive-individualists has been profound. Their academic and scholarly credentials are impressive, and their professional and political "locations" are strategically sound. Though there is no "profession" of possessive-individualists as there is a profession of planners and managers, they nonetheless enjoy a surprising degree of group coherence and identification. It may be fairly said that they now have their own think tank, their own academic departments and institutes. And while their interests certainly range far and wide, we may nonetheless suggest that the peculiar problems of America's cities have particularly held their attention. They represent, then, a third stream of urban political thought which poses a powerful theoretical and practical challenge to those preoccupied with the managerialist-communalist dispute.

BASIC TENETS

Possessive-individualism, as an approach to contemporary urban politics, involves a number of propositions concerning government and politics. Some of these speak directly to managerialist or communalist claims, some do not. As a group, however, they comprise a reasonably coherent and well-integrated ideology of the urban crisis.

1. *Government is, by definition, ill equipped to solve many or even most social problems; indeed, government action often does more harm than good.* In part, this position reflects the possessive-individualists' general cynicism regarding social science and social policy. The realm of social affairs is simply too complex to be broken down, analyzed, and manipulated as the managerialists would suggest; even if policymakers could isolate the causes of social problems, there would be no assurance that particular policies would produce the intended effects. The burgeoning literature on public policy analysis is, in fact, replete with examples of the unintended, even disastrous consequences of well-intentioned policies.

This general position also reflects the belief of possessive-individualists that the causes of social problems would be beyond the reach of even the most enlightened and omniscient government. Sumner's old maxim that "stateways cannot change folkways" is an article of faith among possessive-individualists. In their view, social problems are rooted in the well-established, culturally transmitted social and psychological traits of individuals. Policymakers can build roads, design sewer systems, devise complex tax structures, and the like; they cannot, however, change the way people think and feel and react to the world around them. Our problems lie in our culture, and our culture has a life of its own. Indeed, culture does not reflect government; it is, rather, the other way around.

2. *Nongovernmental factors nonetheless operate to improve the quality of urban life, at least in the long run.* Were it not for this thesis, possessive-individualists would be a gloomy lot indeed. The notion that the public sector is to a significant degree ineffectual is a disheartening one. Fortunately however, certain processes operate beyond the realm of human intentionality to make things better. The inexorable advance of technology would be one such process; certain demographic developments another; the mere assimilation of human experience, yet a third. More generally, possessive-individualists tend to rely heavily on what Robert Nozick calls "invisible-hand explanations" to account for social change and development. In Nozick's words, invisible-hand explanations

> show how some overall pattern or design, which one would have thought had to be produced by an individual's or group's successful attempt to realize the pattern, instead was produced and maintained by a process that in no way had the overall pattern or design "in mind." . . . An invisible-hand explanation explains what looks to be the product of someone's intentional design, as not being brought about by anyone's intentions."[1]

Improvements in living standards, therefore, are likely to be the unplanned and unintended consequences of normal human endeavor, rather than the result of purposive, governmental action.

3. *Of these nongovernmental factors, clearly the most important is the economic marketplace.* Possessive-individualists tend to rely heavily on models roughly inspired by the tradition of classical political economy. Their view is that a vibrant and energetic system of free enterprise is likely to produce more prosperity, generate greater efficiency, and distribute goods more justly than a

system of centralized control, and that this is perhaps especially true of the political economies of metropolitan areas. They also generally adopt Adam Smith's view that monopolies—either in the private or public sector—tend to subvert the healthy operation of the economy.

4. *The notion of the public interest is a sham and ought to be rigorously avoided.* The view that there is an interest or a good that pertains to the community as a whole, that transcends and even undermines the particular interests and passions of private individuals, is basic to *both* managerialism and communalism. As regards urban policy, it suggests that decisions should be made either (a) by a well-trained, scientifically oriented cadre of policymakers held accountable to the people only fitfully and periodically; or (b) by the public itself, in an open and deliberative spirit of self-forgetfulness. For possessive-individualists, on the other hand, the "public interest" is a wild and dangerous phantasm utterly lacking in real-world validity and capable of justifying the most wrong-headed and ill conceived of policies. According to this view, "interests" pertain only to individuals and individuals are, virtually by definition, discrete and idiosyncratic. One can point to this individual or that and say what his or her interests are or might be; but there is, in effect, no "public" to point to. For the public is, according to possessive-individualists, little more than a convenient and artificial agglomeration of individuals; hence, the "public interest" can be, at best, what Rousseau called the sum of particular interests, i.e., a mere aggregation of the needs and desires of individuals.[2]

Indeed, for possessive-individualists the language of the public interest is usually little more than a smokescreen, a device for legitimizing particular policy preferences. A politician who claims that policy X is in the "public interest" is really one who has a personal preference for policy X (i.e., it suits his taste) but who seeks, for practical, political reasons, to cloak that preference in a veil of moral wholesomeness. To be sure, possessive-individualists generally hold out little hope of putting an end to such nonsense. They do, however, hope that at least the thinking public may come to see that urban policy can never be anything but an effort to balance and adjust the competing interests that define the political landscape of the American city.

5. *Thinking effectively about the urban crisis means relying on hard-headed, no-nonsense realism.* In many ways, this is a summary of the first four theses. More often than not, possessive-individualists are self-proclaimed iconoclasts, vigorously attacking and exposing empty shibboleths and vacuous ideals. Though by no means outsiders or antiestablishment types (indeed nothing could be farther from the truth), they are nonetheless grand debunkers, puncturing what they regard as the vain and dangerous idealism of both managerialists and communalists. Rejecting such idealism, they favor sobriety and attention to the facts, a stark and simple realism which alone can identify and begin to deal with the *true* problems of the cities.

Possessive-individualism is certainly stark; the degree to which it is simple and realistic, however, remains to be seen. What is clear is that its impact on urban public policy is, if anything, growing. And this should not be surprising, for it has its roots in some of the most honored and revered sentiments of the American political tradition, especially as embodied in the Constitution itself.

THE AMERICAN TRADITION

In what follows, I wish to argue not that the Constitution is simply an expression or embodiment of possessive-individualism; the sources of the Constitution, and the intentions of the framers, are by no means simple. I do, however, want to show briefly that possessive-individualism is at least a part of the Constitution. And in so doing, I will rely on what is, without doubt, the single most important bit of writing on the Constitution and its meaning, Madison's *Federalist 10*.[3]

Of course, the general argument of *Federalist 10* is too well known to merit much of a summary here. In brief, according to Madison the "principal task of modern legislation" is to somehow cure the "mischiefs of Faction," i.e., the tendency of particularistic interest groups to disrupt the governmental process, undermine stability, and threaten the private rights of individuals.[4] Most dangerous is the possibility that one faction will become a majority faction; for "the superior force of an interested and overbearing majority" is the surest cause of tyranny. There are, says Madison, two general ways of curing the mischiefs of faction: the causes of faction can be removed, or its effects can be controlled. Of course, the latter is the preferred course and, for Madison, that means an "extensive" (i.e., large) society governed by a representative, "republican" constitution.[5]

Even in this simple summary, we can see that the five theses of possessive-individualism are embodied in *Federalist 10*. To begin with, Madison is skeptical regarding the power and efficacy of the public sector. Thus, for example, one way of treating the mischief of faction would involve "giving to every citizen the same opinions, the same passions, and the same interests." Madison rejects this approach as being simply impractical.[6] The opinions, passions, and interests of men are utterly beyond the reach of public policy. Indeed, as long as men remain what they are, discrete individuals whose background, talents, and circumstances vary widely, their attitudes and desires will also vary accordingly. Government must therefore take men as they are and do the best it can.

There is hope, however. For an extensive society—comprised of many regions, different kinds of industry, diverse customs, and the like—will likely be characterized by a multitude of competing factions, thereby making the formation of a majority faction highly unlikely. We have here a variety of "invisible-hand argument." In a large society, many small groups will *naturally* arise and will, of their own accord, *naturally* fail to coalesce into a majority. This happy outcome is not an imposed one, but is produced simply by establishing a structure or a context in which the free and self-interested behavior of individual groups will unconsciously mitigate the danger of tyranny.

Clearly, such groups can be of diverse kinds. But according to Madison, the real causes of faction are economic. Indeed,

> the most common and durable source of factions has been the various and unequal distribution of property. Those who hold and those who are without property have ever formed distinct interests in society. Those who are creditors and those who are debtors, fall under a like discrimination. A landed interest, a manufacturing interest, with many lesser interests, grow up of

necessity in civilized nations, and divide them into different classes, actuated by different sentiments and views.[7]

Thus, the political marketplace, characterized by competition among a multitude of factions, is also an economic marketplace. This is not quite the marketplace of Adam Smith; we can find no systematic and technical analyses of economic relations in *The Federalist Papers*. Nonetheless, for Madison, as for the political economists, the prime mover is economic; and again, given a proper context, the happy though unintended result of such economic competition is peace and prosperity.

It would be wrong to say that Madison has no conception of the common good, for it is in fact a notion that he uses frequently. Nevertheless, his use of it is generally consistent with the viewpoint of possessive-individualists. At least in his mature writings, Madison never seriously considers the notion of a transcendent interest, a public interest over and above and independent of the particular interests of those who constitute society.[8] The "public interest," that is, is best served through the process of group conflict and competition described above. It is, thus, little more than the "sum of particular interests," i.e., a mechanical aggregation that is a far cry from the more sublime notions embraced either by the managerialists or the communalists.

Through all of this, we find unmistakably a self-conscious tone of hard-headed realism. *Federalist 10*, and the other essays of Publius, are exercises in policy analysis which adopt above all an attitude of prudence and pragmatism. Men must be taken as they are; the limits of government must be accepted. The solutions offered may not stir the passions of idealists or touch a responsive chord in the poets among us. The polity envisioned is not, surely, the most attractive one that could be imagined. But imagination is one thing, practicality another. The regime prescribed by Madison, and Hamilton also, may be made up of small, petty people; it may be characterized by incessant competition and disquieting ferment; it may lack that sweet harmony and fraternal loyalty cherished by political thinkers since the beginning of the western tradition. But, in its homely way, it will work to preserve liberty and stave off tyranny at least for a while, and that is the best we can hope for.

This is characteristically in the spirit of possessive-individualism, and is representative of a central tendency of the American political tradition since the founding. Its application to problems of urban politics is thus not surprising. Yet, even with the "discovery" of the urban crisis, it took some time for a possessive-individualist ideology of the urban crisis to develop. For it developed only reactively, as a *response* to the perceived excesses of the managerialists and the communalists respectively, and has thus remained essentially negative in its tone ever since.

In illustrating the specific application of possessive-individualism to contemporary urban politics, I have chosen to examine three books. My claim is not that these are the three best or even most influential examples one could choose. Rather, I would argue that, *taken together*, they summarize the field quite well. As a group, they reflect the major tendencies of possessive-individualism—substantively, theoretically and stylistically—and demonstrate the challenge of possessive-individualism to be a serious one indeed.

The first of our books is Daniel Patrick Moynihan's *Maximum Feasible Misunderstanding*, published in 1969.[9] This book does not offer much in the way of a positive political program. It is essentially an exercise in criticism. Its target is a kind of amalgam of managerialist and communalist ideas, and its substantive focus is the community action part of the War on Poverty. Moynihan's thesis is rather simple: the Community Action Program was an ill-considered venture that reflected certain disturbing tendencies in the making of urban public policy.

In supporting this thesis, Moynihan makes a number of critical observations. The key phrase *maximum feasible participation*, upon which the entire communalist position depended, was not originally a crucial part of the Community Action Program, nor was its meaning very clear. Moreover, the sociological theory upon which the program was based, derived largely from the work of Richard Cloward and Lloyd Ohlin, was hardly universally accepted. In Moynihan's words:

> At any time from 1961 to 1964 an afternoon of library research would have established that the Cloward-Ohlin thesis of

opportunity structure, though eminently respectable, was nonetheless rather a minority position, with the bulk of delinquency theory pointed in quite a different direction. Nor would it have been necessary to have spent an afternoon to ascertain this not unimportant fact. Ohlin would have been pleased to make it explicit in the course of half an hour's conversation.

Those who devised the Community Action Program, and those who approved it, nonetheless went forward with it as though it were a well-justified, scientifically proven solution to problems of the urban poor. The results were, in Moynihan's view, predictably disappointing.

Such an account thus contains really two implicit arguments. First, it contains an attack on communalism, and on the theories of human development and ethics that lie behind it. The Community Action Program failed, that is, precisely because of its misguided communalism. But second, the argument also contains an attack on managerialism. For Moynihan is leery of the idea that public policy should be based on the findings and recommendations of empirical social science. In his own words:

> social science is at its weakest, at its worst, when it offers theories of individual or collective behavior which raise the possibility, by controlling certain inputs, of bringing about mass behavorial change. No such knowledge now exists. Evidence is fragmented, contradictory, incomplete. Enough snake oil has been sold in this Republic to warrant the expectation that public officials will begin reading labels. This precaution, if growing, is nonetheless far from universal.

Of course, Moynihan is himself a social scientist. Thus, he does see an important political role for the social sciences, namely, measuring the impacts of public policies. But his antimanagerialism could not be more evident: the policy proposals of the experts, the social scientists, are so much snake oil, offering illusory solutions to intractable problems. The managerialist's faith in science is replaced by a hard-headed realism in which there may be progress but certainly no panaceas.

If Moynihan's book provides an implicit critique of both

managerial and communal notions by focusing on the War on Poverty, Edward Banfield's *The Unheavenly City* offers a more systematic treatment. It seeks to explain in some depth the nature and sources of urban problems and attempts to account for the failures of managerial and communalist politics.[10] Indeed, Banfield's book is far and away the most celebrated example of neoconservative writing on urban politics. A polemical and inflammatory work, it had been accused of racism and gross insensitivity, and has been classed with the writings of authors such as Jensen and Herrnstein. It is also, in my view, the leading example of the possessive-individualist approach to urban politics.

While many of the criticisms of Banfield concern essentially peripheral matters, the central argument of the book is, in fact, rather simple. Banfield argues (1) that the problems which plague our cities are largely attributable to a relatively small number of the urban poor, (2) that those few troublemakers are incorrigible products of the class culture in which they find themselves, and (3) that there is, unfortunately and for a variety of reasons, very little that can be done about it.

At the core of the argument is a specific and controversial theory of "class culture." In Banfield's view, the cultural traits of individuals can be understood largely in terms of "time-horizon," i.e., "psychological orientation toward the future."[11] Specifically, upper-class individuals have a comparatively long time-horizon. They are "future oriented," hence predisposed to plan for distant, often abstract goals. They are able to put impulses or immediate desires aside, to marshal or invest their resources in the improvement of the future situation, broadly understood. They are, as a result, independent, self-sufficient, creative, socially conscious, productive, and, above all, happy. At the opposite end of the continuum we find Banfield's "lower class." Lower-class individuals are "present oriented" and are, as a result, radically improvident. They are unable to suppress their desires and impulses, hence unable to plan for even the near future. Banfield's description of their specific characteristics has given rise to many of the accusations that his book is racist. In Banfield's view, the lower classes have a "taste for 'action,' " which presumably manifests itself, for example, in violence and in sexual promiscuity.[12] Lower class individuals are also uninterested in holding down jobs for any reasonable period, are careless with their possessions, are filled with self-contempt and feelings of inadequacy, and are especially prone to mental illness.

It should be noted that the concept of class, as used by Banfield, is essentially formal; anyone who is radically present oriented, *regardless of income, race, or social position*, would qualify as a lower-class individual. And indeed, Banfield emphasizes that the vast majority of poor blacks who live in our central-city ghettos are *not* lower-class individuals. The lower-class contingent, rather, constitutes a very small segment of that population. And it is this very small group that is the source of all the truly serious problems of the city, problems that involve not the "amenities" of urban life but, rather, the "essential welfare of individuals" and the "good health of society," problems such as crime, ignorance, and racial tension.[13] And if these troublemakers are overwhelmingly black and poor, that should be regarded not as a condemnation of poor blacks per se (the vast majority of whom are, again, not lower class); it is, rather, attributable to our nation's long and ugly heritage of racial discrimination, together with a complex array of demographic factors.

Indeed, Banfield's notion of class culture is, in large part, a variant of the so-called culture-of-poverty theory which holds that poverty tends to perpetuate itself. The theory is attractive in that it identifies poor people as being caught up in an impersonal vicious circle, a demoralizing syndrome in which the very causes of poverty and its many pathologies tend to be transmitted from generation to generation.[14] The theory is also inflammatory, however, because of its political implications. In particular, it tends to exonerate the dominant political and economic institutions of society. By arguing that poverty tends to perpetuate *itself*, this theory implicity claims that poverty is *not* perpetuated by law, social policy, the corporate structure, and the like. The influence of these latter is thus quite benign; they are not the causes of poverty, nor is their impact in any obvious way malevolent or vicious. Of course, Banfield does not hesitate to identify slavery and our general heritage of racial discrimination as one main reason why so many of the urban lower class happen to be black; he does contend, however, that racial discrimination is on the wane and cannot be considered a major cause of the *perpetuation* of the culture of poverty within the black community.[15]

This view, that the dominant institutions are largely blameless, is only one edge of Banfield's two-edged sword. For we might accept the argument thus far and still advocate vigorous efforts to reform society and break up the culture of poverty. That is, one might agree that public and corporate policy has been largely benign and still argue on humanitarian grounds that policies ought to be changed so as to help our cities' poor.

It is here that we encounter the second edge of the sword. For not only does Banfield contend that the dominant institutions are largely blameless, he also claims that any systematic effort to break up the culture of poverty is doomed to failure. As a good possessive-individualist, his position is that governmental policy must take people as they are; it cannot change by fiat the way people think and feel. In Banfield's words, "no one knows how to change the culture of any part of the population."[16] And even if we could effect such a change, it would only be at such a cost to liberty that the cure would be far more costly than the disease.[17] There are, to be sure, certain policies which might help to *contain*, though surely not cure, the pathological behavior of the urban lower class. Such policies, however, are likely to be politically unacceptable. Indeed, it is the "perversity" of American public opinion, especially the perversity of its "altruistic bias," that prevents reasonable and effective policies from being adopted.[18] Thus, the dominant social and political institutions need not feel guilty about the persistence of poverty in urban America; but even if we did feel moved to do something about the situation, we would find few palatable and effective alternatives. Indeed, conscious efforts to use the public authority to "cure" poverty are likely to do more harm than good.

Banfield's book is, thus, a slashing attack on the exercise of public authority in general. Whether based on managerial or communalist principles, the expansion of the public realm in urban America is for Banfield a prescription for tyranny and for ineffective policy; indeed, the failures of big government only contribute to the already declining sense of authority and legitimacy enjoyed by our public institutions. And again, this would all present an exceedingly gloomy picture except for the fact that things are, in Banfield's view, getting better all the time. In a typical display of possessive-individualist faith, Banfield points to a variety of "imperatives"—technological, demographic, and economic—that operate inexorably to improve the lot of those who live in our cities. The "invisible hands" of various marketplaces—the marketplace of science and ideas, of housing, of goods and services—are in the long run beneficent and effective. Their good work is threatened only by those misguided altruists who would use public power in a futile and dangerous effort to effect radical social change.

It should be noted that Banfield's argument is suffused throughout with an economic kind of reasoning. The actions of individuals are, in large part, attributable to the structure of incentives and disincentives they encounter. We have rioting "mainly for profit" (though also for "fun"); unemployment is, to a significant extent, a structural result of the minimum wage; discipline in the classroom is threatened when employable fourteen- and fifteen-year-olds are forced against their will to stay in school. Given their "cultural" proclivities, men seek fundamentally to maximize utility. The key to public policy then is to structure their relations in such a way that the mischief of selfishness is contained while its more positive effects are nurtured.

To be sure, the economic logic of Banfield's work is largely implicit; he offers no rigorous and systematic analysis of the public economy of urban areas. Such an analysis, however, would be wholly compatible with a possessive-individualist perspective and, indeed, the third book I wish to consider exemplifies this quite well. *Understanding Urban Government* by Robert Bish and Vincent Ostrom has by no means been as influential as Moynihan's book nor as provocative as Banfield's. Nonetheless, it is highly representative of possessive-individualism in its more technical aspect, an aspect which is likely to assume greater importance as the 1980s unfold.[19]

Bish and Ostrom identify their work as being in the tradition of public-choice theory, a theory of decisionmaking which seeks to specify and formalize optimal rules for making intelligent, strategic decisions, including and especially decisions of public consequence. It assumes, among other things, that decisionmakers are rational and self-interested utility maximizers operating under conditions of uncertainty. They are like poker players, each trying to win the pot but ignorant of the cards their opponents are holding. Given the information they *do* have (e.g., their own cards, their opponents' betting decisions, *some* of their opponents' cards as in games of stud poker), they seek the strategy that is most likely to produce a payoff, i.e., that which has the highest "expected utility."

As regards decisions of a public or social nature, however, the situation is rather different from that of a poker game. For many of the goods we seek to get from government are "public goods." Public goods are different from private goods, hence different from poker winnings, in that they are not easily divisible or packageable; individuals cannot be easily excluded from enjoying a public good once it is provided for someone else. Examples would be national defense, clean air, the control of contagious diseases, and the like. If I am well protected from nuclear attack, so is my neighbor, regardless of how much he has contributed to that protection. One implication is that "free riders" cannot be easily excluded from the enjoyment of public goods. If the air is clean, it is clean for all, even those few who have disconnected their catalytic converters.

The broader implications of this general perspective are very complex. As regards the governing of our cities, however, Bish and Ostrom's work is basically a plea for a return to market principles. This means two things. First, it means that many *private goods* currently being provided by one or another governmental entity could be more efficiently and effectively provided by the private sector. Thus, Bish and Ostrom write favorably of "voucher systems" for the provision of education[20] and suggest that private fire-fighting companies can be both more efficient and more responsive in offering fire protection than traditional fire departments.[21] Second, a return to market principles means that certain *public goods* should be provided by public entities *in competition* with one another. Thus, Bish and Ostrom defend the "polycentric" metropolis, i.e., the traditionally fragmented system of metropolitan government in which the metropolitan area is ruled by a crazy quilt of governmental entities including municipalities, counties, special districts, regional councils, and the like. Rather than being inefficient and chaotic, as the managerial tradition holds, the fragmented metropolis is in fact both highly efficient and quite responsive, as various governmental entities compete with one another in providing prospective users with the most attractive and cost-effective package of services.[22]

Again, we can see in Bish and Ostrom's work many of the characteristics of possessive-individualism. There is the skepticism about the public sector in general, especially when it comes to the provision of goods and services. There is the reliance on nongovernmental factors, especially market factors, in the distribution of scarce resources. Further, Bish and Ostrom's work is utterly dependent on economic modes of analysis. Even their partial defense of neighborhood government is made on utterly noncommunalist grounds; although they cite Kotler and others, they favor community control in certain circumstances largely because of its implications for the cost-effective provision of goods and services. Through it all, one finds an unwillingness to dabble in airy ideals; indeed, one encounters a determination to accept people as they are, no matter how uninspiring that might be, and to assemble thereby a reasonably effective and responsible structure of government.

Criticisms of these various works—Moynihan's, Banfield's, Bish and Ostrom's, and others—have been both varied and vehement. Of course, it must be remembered that my grouping such authors together is rather unusual, hence their works are rarely treated as of a piece. Nonetheless, each has been accused of insensitivity, of ignoring the underlying needs and interests of the poor, of offering proposals that work to the further advantage of those already favored by society. And each has been accused of calling for a retreat from the progressive reforms of the postwar era, a return to a meaner time devoid of genuine social conscience. Such criticisms, essentially polemical in nature, may or may not have validity. Indeed, much depends on the technical accuracy of possessive-individualist analyses, and in that sense the proof would be very much in the pudding. If private fire protection companies *do* in fact do a better job, then perhaps Bish and Ostrom's approach in general ought to persuade us. If the consequences of repealing the minimum wage *would* turn out to be largely good, then perhaps we all ought to become closer students of Banfield.

Again, however, I believe a rather different critical strategy is in order.

PREMISES OF POSSESSIVE-INDIVIDUALISM

The term possessive-individualism was employed by C. B. Macpherson in his influential and controversial study of British political thought in the seventeenth century.[23] Macpherson's work has generated considerable criticism and, indeed, there is much in his book with which I strongly disagree. His interpretations of Harrington, the Levelers, and Locke often strike me as one-sided, albeit provocative. There is, however, at least one issue upon which I do agree with Macpherson: the foundation statements of the philosophy of possessive-individualism are to be discovered in the works of Thomas Hobbes.

Hobbes is, of course, the source of many of the most important ideas in modern political thought. His notions of sovereignty and authorization, and of the laws of nature and the social contract, have provided much of the material for such important successors as Locke, Rousseau, and Hegel. It is, however, in his peculiar and distinctive notion of human nature and of man's place in the world that we can find Hobbes's true importance for the tradition of possessive-individualism.

The characteristics of Hobbes's state of nature are generally well known.[24] In the state of nature, life is "solitary, poor, nasty, brutish, and short." This is because men by nature seek gain, safety, and reputation, and do so essentially with recourse to violence. There is no "common power," no government, to hold them in check; nor for that matter are there any moral constraints, since "notions of right and wrong, justice and injustice, have there [in the state of nature] no place." The result, of course, is a war of "every man against every man."

All of this is well known. However, there are certain crucial implications which are perhaps not so well known and which give Hobbes's state of nature its real theoretical identity. To begin with, the individuals who people this natural situation are curiously free from the encumbrances we normally associate with persons who have families, live in cities or villages, read books and exchange ideas, go to church, and the like. They are, in other words, utterly discrete and isolated from one another. They have, as far as we can tell, no past and no culture. Their thoughts are their own, as they are naturally alone, islands unto themselves, atoms. The point is not that they fail to interact, like a bunch of scattered hermits; indeed, Rousseau thought that Hobbes's state of nature was not a true state of nature precisely because it permitted too much interaction. Rather, the point is that each individual brings to these many interactions nothing but himself, uncontaminated as he is by the excess baggage of communal obligations, established cultural values and ideas, interpersonal ties, etc. He is a perfect ingenue, a passionate and rather feverish ingenue to be sure, but one whose motives are ultimately pure and simple and all his own. We may call this the postulate of "atomization."

But what are those motives? What is it that drives and inspires the inhabitants of the state of nature? Hobbes's discussion of the "voluntary motions"—i.e., the passions that prompt men to act—is complex and frequently oversimplified by commentators.[25] Nonetheless, at the risk of distortion we may suggest that, for Hobbes, man in the state of nature is fundamentally an egoist who seeks to maximize those things which have utility for him. He is, quite simply, a possessive individual. The particular things he seeks to possess are various, and go well beyond money. Indeed, power and deference, honor and reputation, perhaps above all else safety, are things which have utility for the individual and which he can have more or less to the exclusion of other people. In any case, the desire for possessions of various sorts is essential for the Hobbesian definition of natural man.

In this picture, at least two sorts of motives are left out. First, Hobbes's natural man is largely unconcerned with what might be called internal attributes, i.e., moral and spiritual qualities such as integrity, conscientiousness, peace of mind, and the like. In Aristotle's terms, he is interested only in "external goods," in possessions.[26] Secondly, Hobbes's natural man is largely unconcerned with the well-being of other sentient creatures including other natural men. Indeed, unlike Rousseau's noble savage, Hobbes's is utterly lacking in natural feelings of sympathy and appears to have no innate sense of community or sociability. His scope of interest is limited to himself, and those he encounters in the world are presumably nothing for him but instruments or obstacles in his quest for useful possessions.

These two characteristics, the concern with external goods and the unconcern with the well-being of others, are precisely what make Hobbes's natural man "possessive" and an "individualist." But there is one other aspect of Hobbes's argument that bears special attention and that points to the particular status of his state-of-nature theory in general. We may call this the postulate of "ahistoricity." The view of human nature that Hobbes presents is utterly ahistorical. Man is *by nature* a possessive individual; and the implication is that this is the case, at least hypothetically, regardless of historical contexts. To be sure, the precise intentions of Hobbes in describing a "state of nature" are unclear. I would suggest that the state of nature is most useful for social theory not as a depiction of some allegedly historical (or prehistorical) period but, rather, as an effort to abstract from observation and experience some essential and underlying truths about human nature. For Hobbes, the fact that man is a possessive individual has nothing to do with history, social circumstances, and the like. Indeed, one gets no sense from *Leviathan* that historical factors play any significant role in the formation of human character. We can perhaps extrapolate from Hobbes and suggest that external circumstances may influence the kinds of possessions individuals find valuable; but there is no sense that man can be anything other than a possessive individual.

Thus, we encounter a threefold formulation: (1) man is discrete and isolated, an island unto himself, at least in psychological terms; (2) as such, he is basically a possessive individual; and (3) this is true regardless of historical circumstance. Clearly the second of these is crucial in rendering the identifying characteristics of human beings and human behavior. But it is also, I would suggest, utterly dependent on the theoretical support of the other two. Were the individual viewed not as a discrete atom but, rather, as an integral part of some higher community which gives to him his place and identity, then the notion of possessive-individualism would be very hard to sustain. It is difficult to imagine individuals deeply bound up with their communities who, at the same time, failed to identify with, and pursue the interests of, those communities. The drone of the beehive can hardly be a possessive individual. Similarly, were historical factors to play a decisive role in the formation of character, then the "fact" of possessive-individualism would have only a provisional, transitory status. That is, were history to change, then the nature of human motivation and behavior might well change accordingly and in dramatic ways. Thus, the threefold nature of Hobbes's formation is, in fact, a unified and mutually sustaining structure: all three propositions are absolutely essential.

Now what is interesting is that the second term of this formulation is to be found in all possessive-individualist analyses of the urban crisis, but not the other two. As has been shown above, the criticisms of Moynihan, the analyses of Bish and Ostrom, the recommendations of Banfield—all are based on the assumption that men are economic beings. In the case of Bish and Ostrom, the assumption is quite explicit, in Moynihan and Banfield rather less so. But the economic logic of all, invoking one or another system of incentives and disincentives designed to produce desired outcomes, is wholly unintelligible without a possessive-individualist view of human nature and human behavior. And, as has also been shown, this view itself is unintelligible without the other two basic postulates, i.e., that of atomization and of ahistoricity.

But what of these other postulates? Here, two things must be noted. First, though their views regarding human nature are virtually unintelligible without them, there is very little in the work of Moynihan and Banfield (for example) that would support the notions of atomization and ahistoricity. Indeed, the general idea of a cycle of poverty, central to the work of both Moynihan and Banfield, would seem to specifically contradict each of these notions. Individuals caught up in a cycle of poverty are presumably deeply affected by familial and communal factors; far from being islands unto themselves, they are in fact products of, and contributors to, an ongoing pattern of social pathology. Moreover, the very concept of such a cycle is laden with historical connotations. Presumably a cycle of poverty is a unique, complex product of historical circumstance; its very status as an identifiable social process suggests its historical specificity, and suggests that other varieties of motivation and behavior are, at least in principle, possible. Thus, the central postulate of possessive-individualism—that humans are possessive individuals—is left hanging in the wind, its natural theoretical supports, atomization and ahistoricity, undermined by the culture-of-poverty argument itself. Indeed, given their tacit rejection of these two postulates, there is no theoretical reason to accept the economic logic of Moynihan and Banfield.

Second, it is nonetheless understandable that these two authors tacitly reject atomization and ahistoricity, for the latter are extremely implausible. The idea that humans are atoms, separate and independent from one another—psychologically and motivationally discrete, as it were—has been criticized by students of politics and society from Hume to de Jouvenel. It is difficult to conceive of individuals utterly free from the influences of family and community, utterly lacking in feelings of sociability and conviviality. If nothing else, the findings of the classical sociologists and their heirs do little to suggest the relevance of this postulate for the study of contemporary politics, including urban politics.

One can say much the same about the postulate of ahistoricity. Since the writings of Herder and Hegel (and Rousseau as well), it is common to see in different historical periods wholly novel and distinctive patterns of human interaction and behavior. For Rousseau, the introduction of private property radically changed human nature;[27] for Hegel, the successive unfolding of *Geist* is associated with fundamentally different types of culture and largely unprecedented kinds of motivation.[28] The notion that human nature is utterly fixed and largely immune from the effects of historical circumstance is thus no longer very credible.

It should be noted that these criticisms have little bearing on the work of Hobbes himself. For Hobbes was engaged in an abstract, deductive enterprise designed to show how the exercise of coercive political authority can be morally justified. His philosophy thus invokes the state of nature and its associated postulates as mere working hypotheses, tentative and provisional. *If* humans were possessive individuals, he asks, what then would be the consequences for political right? Contemporary possessive-individualists, on the other hand, ask a different, rather less compelling question: *Since* humans *are* possessive individuals, what then are the consequences for urban public policy? Such misguided realism, rejected by much of modern social theory, is in stark contrast to the more plausible and persuasive use of the state of nature by another contemporary writer, Robert Nozick. For Nozick, the state of nature is but a convenient fiction, useful in making a logical argument but hardly a description of the way men are or ever were.[29] The contrast with the work of (say) Bish and Ostrom is notable.

In sum, the basic premises of possessive-individualism are difficult to sustain. The authors we are considering either accept the most dubious principles of atomization and ahistoricity or else assume, without foundation or support, a possessive-individualist view of human nature. Either way, the policy consequences are profound. For by holding to so fixed and narrow a conception of human motivation and behavior, possessive-individualist theorists of the urban crisis necessarily reject communalist and managerial politics altogether. They reject, that is, the notion that the citizens of our great urban centers can be reoriented and redirected toward serving the public interest. And again, the persuasiveness of this rejection is only as great as the persuasiveness of the ideas upon which it is based.

INDIVIDUAL RIGHTS

Historically, those who accept the premises of possessive-individualism have gone on to articulate a single and extraordinarily influential ethical idea, namely, the notion that human beings possess natural and inalienable rights. Indeed, the natural rights tradition is virtually unthinkable without the above-mentioned assumptions regarding man and man's place in the world. Briefly, according to this tradition humans have certain rights which are inviolable and which are the necessary conditions for living a truly human existence. Such a view requires that individuals be regarded, at least in moral terms, as discrete and separate, each possessing his *own* rights and immunities. Such a view also requires that those rights and immunities attend to him not for any contingent or circumstantial reason, not because of history, but simply and solely because he happens to be a human. And finally, such a view implies that men will in fact enjoy their rights, will want to have them and exploit them so as to live a more prosperous and contented life.

The natural rights tradition is a central part of the possessive-individualist approach to contemporary urban politics. At base, the writers we have discussed assume, explicitly or implicitly, that the protection of certain natural rights is a fundamental purpose of government. And among these rights, the most central, and the one most in need of protection, is the right to own property—to have one's possession of things, and one's ability to dispose of those possessions, acknowledged and sanctioned. Man is, by nature, a possessive individual. Thus, if he is to be permitted to live according to his nature, then his ability to possess things and to exclude others from the things he does possess must be recognized and preserved. It is this constraint which defines the parameters within which the urban crisis must be approached. Indeed, the failure to duly acknowledge the right to property is itself a central cause of the urban crisis. Misguided policies aimed at land-use planning, income redistribution, and the housing supply have induced the flight of the middle classes from the central city, thereby robbing it of its social and fiscal strength; governmental paternalism has turned the urban poor into an enervated dependent class, unable to help itself and deprived of its purpose and dignity; government consolidation and bureaucratization has undermined the operation of the urban political marketplace, creating gross inefficiencies that drain the capacities of the public weal. In each case, interfering with natural economic processes has created a perverse structure of incentives and disincentives destined to exacerbate the problems of the metropolis.

Clearly the natural rights tradition is a venerable one, hallowed in the great documents of America's founding. To be more precise, however, there are at least two natural rights traditions, one of them rather more persuasive than the other. Which of these has had the greater influence on contemporary urbanists is by no means clear. But in either case, the notion of natural rights presents theoretical difficulties which, in and of themselves, lead us to doubt the adequacy of possessive-individualism per se.

One tradition of natural rights discourse can be traced, again, to the writings of Hobbes. As in so many other cases, Hobbes's discussion of rights and of natural law is notable for its clarity and reasonableness.[30] For Hobbes, the fundamental right of nature is "the liberty each man has to his own power, as he will himself, for the preservation of his own nature." Attendant to this right are the various laws of nature. These are general rules, discovered by reason, "by which a man is forbidden to do that which is destructive of his life or takes away the means of preserving the same and to omit that by which he thinks it may be best preserved." Among the laws of nature are that men ought to endeavor peace, perform their covenants, accommodate themselves to one another, and the like. Importantly, these laws are understood by Hobbes to be merely "convenient articles of peace." They are discoverable by "reason," by which Hobbes means not an inquiry into the metaphysical nature of things but rather, and more simply, the reckoning of consequences. It is reason in the sense of means-ends reasoning.[31] And thus, while Hobbes does concede that the laws of nature might be the commands of God, he emphasizes rather the fact that they "are but conclusions or theorems concerning what conduces to the conservation and defense of themselves [i.e., humans]."

What should be emphasized, then, is the hypothetical character of natural rights and laws. For Hobbes, such rights and laws have no transcendent or extrahuman status. Indeed, his use of the word natural in this context seems to me awkward and inappropriate, as though he were forced to use an outmoded vocabulary to express novel ideas. For the natural rights and laws he mentions are in fact nothing more than the instruments of prudence. They have moral force only insofar as they work to the benefit of individuals.

In contrast, we must also consider what might be called the Lockeian tradition of natural rights. It is conventional to lump Locke's political thought together with that of Hobbes and to identify them together as the great systematizers of Western liberalism. In fact, however, their theories are profoundly different, and that difference manifests itself most clearly as regards natural rights and laws. Whereas for Hobbes such rights and laws are mere precepts of reason and prudence, for Locke they are in fact elements of a higher law, God's law if you will, and hence have a transcendent, metaphysical status. Whereas Hobbes's state of nature is an amoral realm in which each person has a right to anything and everything, Locke's is governed by an antecedent and immutable moral code, the violation of which is equivalent to sin.

According to Locke,

> The state of nature has a law of nature to govern it, which obliges every one; and reason, which is that law, teaches all mankind who will but consult it that, being all equal and independent, no one ought to harm another in his life, health, liberty, or possessions.[32]

Attendant to this is the fundamental natural right:

> the execution of the law of nature is, in that state, put into every man's hands, whereby everyone has a right to punish the transgressors of that law to such a degree as may hinder its violation.[33]

While the substance of these formulations may not be very different from those of Hobbes, the theory behind them is. For whereas Hobbes's notions are conceived of as the products of rational calculation, Locke's are written in stone, are expressive of an eternal and immutable code of ethics, divine in origin. And thus, while Hobbes uses an obsolete Thomistic vocabulary to express new ideas, Locke uses the same vocabulary to defend an essentially Thomistic theory.

The usual political concomitant of natural rights theory, in either of its versions, is a commitment to what Isaiah Berlin referred to as the idea of negative liberty.[34] In brief, this is the idea that political freedom means "freedom from" some external constraint. The free individual is the individual who is left alone to as great a degree as possible, and who is thus free to do what he pleases provided that he does not interfere with similar freedom for other individuals. And he enjoys this freedom largely because he has a right to it. In contrast, the notion of positive liberty means freedom to do something specific, for example, to be a good citizen or to realize one's potential to the fullest. Whereas the institutional implications of positive liberty are complex and open to much dispute, negative liberty generally involves a defense of limited government. That is, the role of government is said to be limited to the protection of the individual's natural right to freedom from external interference. Its purpose is to create a safe context in which individuals can live their lives the way they want to.

Now virtually all possessive-individualists accept this notion of negative liberty and limited government. But again, whether they do so on Hobbesian or Lockeian grounds is by no means clear. Many possessive-individualists appear to defend their position with largely utilitarian (i.e., Hobbesian) arguments. Thus, for example, some of Milton Friedman's arguments in favor of market mechanisms are based largely on questions of efficiency, i.e., the market is simply a more *efficient* allocator of goods and services, hence is more conducive to prosperity.[35] This form of argument can be easily traced in the possessive-individualists' writings on urban affairs, and it is utterly consonant with their self-proclaimed, hard-headed realism. However, there are at least two difficulties with this view, both of which have been treated more closely in Chapter 2. Briefly, systems of utilitarianism are dependent on the kinds of goods deemed useful. It may well be that market mechanisms and limited government are uniquely able to confer certain kinds of benefits; but it may also be that other kinds of benefits—benefits not conferred by, perhaps even undermined by, the free market—are found to be even more valuable. Such things as equality, a sense of security and belonging, the maximization of human potential, and the like, are things which humans have historically valued and which, many would claim, are subverted by the ideas and structures of possessive-individualism. Further, it is by no means obvious that market mechanisms are necessarily superior in terms of efficiency. To a great extent the argument is merely an empirical one. Do markets in fact distribute goods more efficiently than more directed forms of social action? Thus, a strictly utilitarian view means that natural rights and limited government ought to be preserved only as long as the evidence proves their necessary relationship to prosperity and efficiency. If it could be shown that central economic planning, or even some form of totalitarian control, could generate greater utility, however defined, then the notion of natural rights would have to be jettisoned. Indeed, Hobbes himself drew political conclusions from his utilitarian premises that were by no means completely compatible with the theory of negative liberty. The Hobbesian tradition thus offers no firm ground for the belief in limited government.

As a result, possessive-individualists, in spite of their instinctive utilitarianism, have frequently sought refuge in the Lockeian tradition. The natural rights of man are, in some sense, self-evident. They are given, are part of what it means to be a human, hence have an inviolable, even sacred status. If we know anything, it is that such rights exist and must be protected above all else. This kind of argument is, in fact, even less satisfying than the other. For it forces possessive-individualists to adopt a kind of mysticism, to fall back on a variety of fideism that utterly belies their commitment to hard-headed, realistic analysis. Indeed, the view that men have certain "natural" rights apart from any kind of human convention can be nothing other than an article of faith, something which can be asserted but hardly demonstrated. Where do such rights come from? How did we get them? Under what circumstances can they be circumvented? Locke himself failed to provide anything even approaching a satisfying answer to such questions. Indeed, the possessive-individualist view that property rights are natural rights is especially controversial; the entire Marxist tradition is founded, at least in part, on the view that private property is merely conventional and is, as such, a fundamental source of human repression and exploitation.

The theory of possessive-individualism thus finds itself without firm theoretical supports. As we have seen, the view of man that it promotes—with its notions of atomization and ahistoricity—is difficult to sustain. And its philosophy of natural rights amounts less to a moral theory than to a surrogate for moral theory, a set of weakly defended postulates upon which broad ethical judgments are to be based. As a result, its fundamental political principles, involving notions of limited government and negative liberty, fail to carry the kind of intellectual weight that the purveyors of possessive-individualism would have us believe.

The managerialist-communalist debate is thus not solved by possessive-individualism. We have three important and influential ideologies of urban politics, each of which seems plausible at first but which can be shown to rest on dubious premises. We need a theory of urban politics that responds to immediate, practical concerns but that, at the same time, satisfies our intellectual sensibilites. We cannot here construct such a theory. But we can perhaps describe some of the relevant factors that such a theory should consider, and suggest some of the broader premises that such a theory might invoke. It is to this task that we now turn.

5. TOWARD A PHILOSOPHY OF URBAN POLITICS

The "crisis of the cities" has manifested itself in numerous ways. New York and Cleveland have faced bankruptcy. Air quality in the Los Angeles basin continues to be alarmingly bad. With the demise of the Daley machine, Chicago finds itself confronting a political civil war. Newark is plagued by a decaying physical infrastructure, Houston by a chaotic and irrational process of development, Detroit by a staggering crime rate. In Boston and Miami, racial tensions rise and fall like the tides. And in other cities across America we seem to encounter an unending parade of crises: public employee strikes, police scandals, outbreaks of violence in the schools, widespread homelessness, and the like. Even where efforts at gentrification and inner-city revitalization have met with success, the lot of the urban poor seems hardly to have improved from the pre-riot years.

Problems such as these are obviously difficult, perhaps even insoluble. We do not yet know how to lower the crime rate, end racism, educate all of our children, or clean up our cities. One result of this is that the war on such problems has been fought largely in pragmatic terms. Policymakers have confronted problems as they appear, improvising responses to them in a more or less unsystematic manner, retaining or revising policies on the basis of short-term substantive and political consequences. And given the uncertainties of the world in which we live, this is perhaps as it should be.

Nonetheless, policymakers do not generally operate in an intellectual vacuum. Whether they know it or not, those responsible for making decisions in urban politics are influenced by general systems of thought—orientations or perspectives—which shape the way in which questions are asked, and which favor certain options over others. Stated otherwise, urban politics is deeply ideological. Decisions and policies are the products of, and must be rationalized and defended in terms of, idea systems—however tacit and inchoate—which, as a consequence of this, take on special importance.

The arguments of the foregoing chapters are therefore of practical as well as theoretical significance. Indeed, implicit in my approach has been the assumption that our three ideologies—managerialism, communalism, and possessive-individualism—set the substantive parameters of urban politics in general. There is, that is to say, an ongoing dialogue among these three sets of ideas which informs and influences the perhaps more prosaic debates concerning the crisis of the cities. Communalism is, at base, a comment on managerialism, and the managerialists have responded in turn. Possessive-individualists, meanwhile, have looked at the other two and have rejected both of them; indeed, much of possessive-individualism is largely a running criticism of managerialism and communalism.

And while this dialogue may at times seem abstract, the more tangible implications of it are never very far from the surface. Such implications have to do with the style of urban governance (e. g., professional versus amateur democracy). They also concern specific policies having an immediate and concrete impact (methods of law enforcement, the distribution of services to the poor, etc.). They involve more general interpretations of the urban crisis itself and ask to what extent it really is a crisis. Indeed, most debates concerning urban policies are understandable precisely in the ideological terms we have described.

Thus, for example, seemingly mundane controversies concerning urban highway systems often take shape as battles between managerial and communalist principles. Managerialists tend to look at the evidence concerning traffic patterns, demographic factors, prospects for economic development, and the like, and on this basis attempt to pursue optimal transportation policies. While they may also seek to consider and appease neighborhood concerns, these are usually viewed as just one more variable—often a minor variable—in the overall policy equation. Communalists, on the other hand, tend to see such highway projects as potential neighborhood threats—breaking up communities, isolating them in an unnatural way, and undermining their character by facilitating undesirable kinds of access. For them, the sense of community is a fragile and precious thing, and should not be treated as just another consideration to be faced by decisionmakers.[1]

School desegregation controversies can similarly be understood in managerial versus communalist terms. Proponents of forced busing, for example, invoke elevated considerations of the "public interest" in seeking the quickest and most effective means of desegregating schools. A number of key federal court opinions are typical in this regard. Opponents, on the other hand, both black and white, often argue in communalist terms, emphasizing the importance of neighborhood schools as both socializing and civic institutions.[2]

Possessive-individualists, of course, offer rather different kinds of policy prescriptions. Their faith is in the invisible hand that guides urban America; the comprehensive plans of managerialism and the neighborhood governments of communalism are equally fatuous. When a problem becomes *really* a problem, then something *will* be done about it, if at all possible; though of course, some problems are utterly intractable and must simply be endured. Thus, for example, we have Banfield suggesting that urban air pollution is not truly serious since people are unwilling to pay the price of having it eliminated; Moynihan despairs of fighting a successful war on poverty because we simply do not know how to fight such a war; Bish and Ostrom suggest that certain key services, such as fire protection, can be best provided by the private sector. In some ways, the culmination of these views was to be found in the Reagan administration's original national urban policy, with its effort to retrench social services programs, its appeal to private sources of philanthropy, and its focus on "enterprise zones" designed to stimulate economic activity in depressed urban areas.

Now there is clearly a sense in which these ideologically based disputes seem to miss the point. For it would appear that all three perspectives contribute something important to an understanding of the urban crisis and its resolution. Few would deny that we need some kind of planning component in the urban decisionmaking process. Nearly everyone would agree that a sense of community can contribute greatly to the political and social well-being of our urban centers. And one can hardly gainsay the utility of hard-headed realism when considering specific proposals designed to solve difficult and complex problems.

But it is when a mere planning component becomes full-blooded managerialism, when an interest in the sense of community turns into communalism, when hard-headed realism appears as doctrinaire possessive-individualism that we get into trouble. In short, when attitudes and orientations solidify into ideologies, however unspecified and diffuse, the chances of irresolvable conflict increase greatly. There may seem to be something perverse and unnatural about this; if only we could prevent the development of ideas into ideologies, the essential compatibility of seemingly different opinions would become so much more evident. Yet I would suggest that the tendency to operate in ideological terms is virtually inevitable. For it appears to be a basic property of human thinking that we seek to make coherent our apparently random thoughts, to systematize them or organize them so that they make more sense, so that we have not merely random thoughts but, rather, a systematic position. And there is, perhaps paradoxically, a good deal of virtue in this. For while ideological thinking may intensify conflict, it also makes latent oppositions manifest and, thus, forces us to deal with them. Again, a communalist can well admit the necessity of a managerial component in urban society. But the fact remains that the underlying intellectual premises of communalism contradict those of managerialism, and that contradiction is ultimately decisive.

All of which is to suggest the practical, day-to-day relevance of ideologies of the urban crisis. An understanding of the perspectives we have discussed, and of their interrelationships, is a key to understanding concrete proposals offered as solutions to the various problems of our cities. It becomes important, therefore, to assess the strengths and weaknesses of urban ideologies, both vis-á-vis one another and on their own merits. At this stage, then, it will be useful to reprise our earlier judgments of the three ideologies and to offer a more general evaluation. Given such an evaluation, we may then begin to move toward a more satisfying approach to the urban crisis.

THE LIMITS OF URBAN IDEOLOGY

As we have seen, there is a good deal to be said against each of the ideologies. Each has special features which make it unattractive, features which are not unessential but in fact definitive. As indicated above, the positivist epistemology and utilitarian ethics of managerialism no longer seem very persuasive. Many philosophers of science now agree that the methods of the natural sciences are not suitable to the analysis of social relations; indeed, even the hard sciences do not seem to proceed according to the older positivist canon. Similarly, moral theorists are increasingly convinced that ethical positions cannot be reduced to simple questions of taste and preference; such positions must, therefore, be open to genuine critical scrutiny and evaluation. Against communalism it is widely argued that urbanites are in fact no more alienated than anyone else, hence the peculiarities of the urban crisis cannot be simply attributed to the decline of community. Moreover, there is little evidence to indicate that experiments in neighborhood government have in any way improved the civic capacities of those involved; indeed, the relationship between political involvement and sociological factors such as community is still a matter of considerable dispute.[3]

Against possessive-individualism it is argued that the postulates of atomism and ahistoricity are implausible and unpersuasive; even certain of the possessive-individualists seem to reject them. Further, possessive-individualism has little positive to say about social justice; it clings to the dubious notion that the putative efficiency of the marketplace more than compensates for skewed distributive outcomes.

Such criticisms are weighty and well worth considering. They raise serious questions about the three ideologies, hence about policies and processes based on them. But for now, I wish to concentrate on two further problems which are more generally relevant to the issue of ideology and urban politics, problems which our three perspectives share in roughly equal measure.

1. To begin with, each of the ideologies of urban politics is insufficiently urban. By this I mean to say that there is nothing that especially suits them to the unique and particular issues of *city* politics. What we want is an approach that responds specifically to the distinctive role of urban government in the federal system and focuses thereby on the peculiar problems and potential of the city. None of the three ideologies does this.

Indeed, managerialism, communalism, and possessive-individualism are curiously alike in offering views that actually threaten the meaningful existence of the city as polity. For managerialists, the city is not simply an enterprise association; it is, rather, just one subsidiary of a much larger enterprise association. Its value thus depends entirely on the degree to which it efficiently pursues a "public interest" established at higher levels, i.e., in the state capitols or in Washington, D.C. As such, its status is—at least in theory—quite shaky. That is to say, the degree to which an independent city government can contribute effectively to managerialist goals is an open question. Such managerial principles as centralization, hierarchy, and formal coordination might well suggest that we would do better to strip the city of its policymaking prerogatives and turn it into what it seems increasingly to be anyway—merely an administrative arm of the state.[4]

Communalism presents an even greater threat to the city. In its Jeffersonianism, its cult of smallness, its emphasis on face-to-face intimacy, communalism implicitly holds that an authentic politics is possible only at the neighborhood level, thereby casting doubt on the possibility of a genuine *city* politics. Further, the notion that legitimate authority should devolve to the neighborhood betrays the view that there are no peculiar problems, and no special opportunities, to be found in America's urban areas qua metropolitan regions.

Much the same can be said for possessive-individualism. Implicit in possessive-individualism is the view that people who live in cities face problems that are only superficially unique. All of us—whether we live in cities, suburbs, or rural areas—are economic beings, and the process of public choice that operates in nonurban settings is generally the same as that characteristic of the city.

Ultimately, then, there is nothing particularly "urban" about the three ideologies of the urban crisis. This would not be a problem if, in fact, there were nothing distinctive about urban politics. Our intuitions tell us otherwise, however. We seem convinced that the ecological, economic, demographic, and purely physical nature of the city makes it a unique setting for social interaction, and provides obstacles and opportunities that are qualitatively different from those found elsewhere. Assuming this to be true, then, we need a philosophy of politics that is explicitly responsive to the peculiarities of urban areas.

2. Our three ideologies are also insufficiently abstract. Now this is a criticism that many authors would actually welcome. The scientific practicality of the managerialists, the down-to-earth populism of the communalists, the hard-headed realism of the possessive-individualists—these would seem to be virtues rather than vices.

When we look for normative theories of politics, however, we look for standards of moral judgment that transcend particular circumstances. This is not to say that we require the discovery and elucidation of eternal laws of right and wrong. It is, however, to say that we need principles that are true not merely contingently but categorically, principles formulated not to scratch particular itches but to reflect broad ethical judgments. An adequate approach to the urban crisis should treat the specific and particular problems of our cities, but should do so in terms of general moral principles which are justified on rational, rather than empirical, grounds.

Managerialism is justified largely by examining the allegedly manifest evils of interest-group liberalism, i.e., a pluralist politics based on competition, negotiation, and compromise among the manifold organized interests in the city. It considers the bad consequences of politics-as-usual, and proceeds from there to the putatively self-evident truths of science and utility. Communalism is based on the presumed alienation of the urban masses, and proposes against it the simple solution of neighborhood democracy. Possessive-individualism takes a hard look at the unintended consequences of government action, and suggests a return to a simpler, market-oriented mode of decisionmaking. In each case, prescriptions are rooted largely in empirical considerations. A particular empirical fact of the urban environment is shown to be troubling, and an alternative is somehow devised. Ultimately, then, there is no sense that these ideologies are really driven by a more general vision of right and wrong.

It may well be that a government of managers would produce more effective policies; but does that constitute a sufficient justification for managerial government? Perhaps sound policies are not the only relevant criteria of good government. Do the ennobling and unifying consequences of communalism outweigh the potential threat, mentioned above, to the freedom of the individual? Perhaps freedom (in the negative sense) is more valuable than public-spiritedness. And why should we prefer the putative efficiency of the marketplace to the hoped-for equality of nonmarket systems? Perhaps prosperity is less important than justice.

It may seem paradoxical to pose these two sets of criticisms—that the ideologies are both insufficiently urban and insufficiently abstract—against the authors we have been considering. On the one hand, we seem to be criticizing them for being too general, on the other hand for not being general enough. In fact, though, the issue is quite different. We may say that all ideologies invoke two different intellectual operations, the adoption of *standards of judgment* (i.e., yardsticks by which to measure good and bad, right and wrong) and the application of those standards to particular *spheres of political life.* A sensible approach would be to adopt *general* standards of judgment which have some kind of independent basis and justification, and then apply them to *particular* spheres of political life, which presumably have unique and distinctive problems. But our ideologies appear to have proceeded the opposite way: they have adopted standards based largely on the particular, empirical problems of urban America and then have formulated strategies of application which are not particularly geared to the special nature of the problems involved. It is thus hard to see why we should be compelled either by the standards invoked or by the strategies suggested.

We seek an approach to the urban crisis, then, that is truly urban, that recognizes the distinctive potential of the city, and that does so in terms of rational principles that can be argued and justified on their own grounds, apart from particular empirical considerations. In short, we seek a body of thought that more closely approaches the category of *political philosophy* as outlined in the first chapter of this book.

EMERGENT APPROACHES: NEO-MARXISM

In the past several years, two bodies of literature have emerged which are largely free of the problems just mentioned and which perhaps point toward a philosophy, rather than an ideology, of urban politics. One such approach is frankly Marxist in orientation and seeks to understand the city in terms of the social processes of postindustrial capitalism. The other is, perhaps, more Aristotelian in temper—though not necessarily in doctrine—and seeks to recapture the notion of the city as a locus of moral discourse. These approaches are philosophical rather than ideological—as here defined—in part because they self-consciously invoke standards of judgment presumed to be relatively universal in application; their evaluations, that is, are framed not in terms of solving this or that particular problem but rather in terms of some larger ethical principle. They are only emergent approaches, however, in that their actual influence on urban politics has thus far been negligible. One would have a great deal of trouble pointing to urban policies or institutions based directly on Marxist or Aristotelian principles. Still, the intellectual power of these approaches, and their potential for resolving some of the difficulties mentioned earlier, make them worthy of our consideration.

Perhaps the foremost exponent of a Marxist theory of the city is Manuel Castells. Castells's *The Urban Question*, originally published in French in 1972 but not translated until 1977, is a rambling, turgidly written, but nonetheless impressive treatment of a broad range of urban literatures dealing with the history of cities, spatial development, urban culture, politics, planning, and the like.[5] It adopts a comparative perspective, and treats of urban life not only in Western Europe and the United States but also in socialist countries and the Third World (especially Latin America). Though ostensibly a work of

Marxist sociology, Castells's book has clear enough implications for a normative theory of the urban crisis.

Castells's goal is to generate theoretical materials which can help to account for the "urban form" in a spatial/geographic sense, to explain also the particular cultural traits of urban social life, and finally to outline the bases of urban politics and political conflict. He adopts a "structural" Marxism developed most notably by Louis Althusser and employed most brilliantly by Nicos Poulantzas. According to this formulation, the determinant of social life is something called the "social formation" which is a structure of institutions and relationships roughly classifiable into three kinds: the economic, the political, and the ideological. The economic refers essentially to the production and consumption of commodities, the political to the activities of the state, the ideological to such cultural forms as art, religion, and entertainment. There is a certain autonomy to these regions of human endeavor. Althusserians reject the simple economic determinism of the so-called vulgar Marxists; the activities of the state, for example, are not simply reducible to the influence of economic forces but may, indeed, have an independent impact on the operation of the economy itself. Still, in any particular historical setting, the activities of the three regions coalesce into a single structure—the social formation—the character of which is ultimately reflective of economic processes and institutions. That is, economic forces are determinative "in the last analysis."[6]

Although Castells spends a great deal of time analyzing the "ideological" character of much urban sociology, and even wonders about the validity of the category *urban* itself, the most exciting part of his book involves an attempt to illustrate how the structuralist concept of a social formation might be useful in explaining the problems of the city. Castells seeks to demonstrate, in a suggestive rather than conclusive manner, how various aspects of the urban form can be understood in terms of the productive/consumptive, political/administrative, ideological/cultural needs of postindustrial capitalism. According to Castells, the city plays a particular and special functional role in the operation of the capitalist system involving the reproduction of the work force; its problems, therefore, are entirely traceable to the economic, political, and ideological structure of American capitalism. Unlike radical theorists of the community power debate—notably Floyd Hunter and William Domhoff—Castells seeks to explain urban outcomes not in terms of the semiconspiratorial activities of an economic elite, but rather in terms of the natural structural/functional requirements of the capitalist system.

Castells's specific analyses are highly formalized and schematic. There are, however, numerous other examples of a Marxist perspective being effectively used to account for some particular facet of urban politics. Thus, for instance, John H. Mollenkopf considers the postwar politics of urban redevelopment and traces its various problems to the economic and administrative needs of capitalism.[7] According to Mollenkopf, urban renewal had its roots in a postwar urban crisis involving the loss of population to the suburbs, expanding black slums, and a consequent dramatic decline in central-city land values. He traces these problems in large part to the competitive realities of the economy and the corporate need for stable and orderly productive environments. The crisis, however, was extremely damaging to certain other corporate sectors, and the result was a progrowth movement aimed at restoring the central-city infrastructure. But the very success of this movement in turn generated another urban crisis as neighborhoods, especially poor ones, reacted sometimes violently to the disruptive effects of urban renewal. Throughout, Mollenkopf emphasizes the interdependence of the urban and capitalist structures:

> Above all, cities are a social and political device for creating the cohesive, ordered environment necessary for combining labor and capital effectively. . . . The relationship between the economy and urban institutions should not, however, be construed as one of simple determinism. [T]he economy itself could not function without an adequate and cohesive set of social and political institutions to concentrate and mobilize human and physical capital.

Similarly, Richard Child Hill analyzes the recent fiscal problems of the city in terms of the structural exigencies of contemporary capitalism. In Hill's formulation, the modern economy requires large-scale "social capital outlays" which are required for "capital accumulation and are indirectly productive of private profit." Stated otherwise, the economic substructure requires a vigorous public sector which will act to ensure the reproduction of a large yet quiescent force of human capital. As a result, capitalism demands an expanded social services role for local governments. But perhaps paradoxically, the same system also facilitates a distribution of wealth such that cities are financially unable to fulfill that role. The result is a structural contradiction manifesting itself in the fiscal insolvency of municipal corporations. Hill sums up the perspective nicely:

> The city is forged upon the hearth of a given mode of production. . . . A particular city cannot be divorced from the encompassing political economy within which it is embedded and through which it manifests its particular functions and form. . . . Crucial to understanding the urban fiscal crisis is awareness of the role the city plays as a form of government, a vital component of the capitalist state.[8]

Of course, such analyses are based on an explicit and self-conscious set of premises derived from Marx. While authors often disagree seriously in their reading of Marx, they all pretty much adopt in one form or another certain fundamentals of dialectical materialism: the modern economy is based on the separation of labor and capital; this separation is responsible for the division of society into classes; capitalism is a system geared toward the accumulation of surplus value; the course of history is rooted in the forces and relations of production and is propelled by the development of internal contradictions which manifest themselves in class struggle. Implicit in all of this is an overriding normative judgment: the crisis of the cities, rooted as it is in the dominant system of production and consumption, cannot be solved unless that system is somehow changed. Urban problems can be addressed, that is, only through a radical restructuring of the larger society's basic institutions.

We may well disagree with such a judgment. But it has the advantage of being derived from philosophic positions which are explicit, accesssible, and systematically defended. The body of Marxist thought, from the writings of Marx himself to those of Engels, Lenin, Lukács and beyond, is open for our inspection and analysis. It would be wrong to minimize the philosophical differences between various Marxist traditions. But we can nonetheless see that neo-Marxist approaches to the urban crisis are based on a clear and common set of principles which can be discussed, debated, and evaluated.

EMERGENT APPROACHES: THE CITY AS POLITY

A very different kind of approach to urban politics is evident in the recent book by Hadley Arkes, *The Philosopher in the City*.[9] Arkes looks at five general areas of urban politics: urban protest behavior, public education, the urban decisionmaking process, housing, and the regulation of vice. He offers a number of judgments in these areas which are extremely controversial and provocative. He argues for significant limits on the scope of free speech in public places, supports the notion of "group libel," criticizes those who advocate community control of schools, finds much recent Supreme Court doctrine on forced busing to be intellectually indefensible, favors the political machine over many so-called reform structures, and supports in principle the regulation of morals. In the 1980's, we would call Arkes a conservative, though it is clearly not the conservatism of a Banfield or a Milton Friedman.

Arkes's specific positions, however, are less important for our purposes than the overall nature of his project. His goal, perhaps more than anything else, is to view the problems of the city as moral problems and to insist that the effort to deal with them must be undertaken in terms of ethical principles. He rejects solutions which are based on contingent, empirical considerations—e.g., "We must have busing because the psychosocial effects of segregation are thus and so"—and argues, roughly in Kantian terms, that policy must be "established on a ground of principle that cannot be evaded." His book is largely a search for such principles and an attempt to apply them to the problems of the city.

Implicit in this project is the view that urban issues are uniquely urban. The problems that Arkes deals with are problems that affect city life as they affect life nowhere else. Thus, the issue of protest behavior and public disorder does not typically arise in rural areas; it is a distinctly metropolitan phenomenon. Similarly, the problem of "combat zones" where vice is tolerated is a characteristically urban problem. But against such problems, Arkes seeks to pose solutions based on more general, abstract principles of right and wrong, principles sanctioned by something like the Kantian categorical imperative.

Also implicit in Arkes's work is the notion that the city is not simply an enterprise association, or a formless aggregation of neighborhoods, or a convenient structure in which to pursue individual economic goals. Rather, Arkes seems to hold the view, largely Aristotelian in origin, that the city is best understood as a "polity," a locus of citizenship in which individuals can engage in a process of deliberation and discussion aimed at pursuing a public interest that accords with basic moral judgments or intuitions. There is nothing inherently conservative in this; it simply reflects a determination to take the city seriously as an object of philosophic interest.

Regrettably, the specific principles upon which Arkes's conclusions rest never emerge very clearly. He opposes his Kantianism to certain varieties of utilitarianism, but rejects utilitarianism on no very clear grounds. Further, when Arkes declares this or that to be right or wrong, it is not entirely obvious what standards he has invoked. Unlike the neo-Marxists, Arkes appears to offer no "ontology"—i.e., no underlying notion of how the world works and what man's proper role in that world is. Even basic Kantian premises regarding rationality, the will, and human autonomy are largely ignored. Still, for our purposes Arkes's insistence that urban problems be approached in terms of basic moral principles is more important than the fact that his book fails to supply such principles.

Far less ambitious, but in some respects as useful, is a recent essay by Richard Dagger on the city as polity.[10] Dagger bases the crisis of the cities on their failure to encourage the practice of citizenship. He understands citizenship in an explicitly Aristotelian sense:

the true citizen plays a full and active part in the affairs of his or her community. [But] the character or nature of one's participation also counts. [I]t carries with it a responsibility to act with the interest of the community in mind.

This may remind us of certain communalist themes, but in fact the differences are profound. For Aristotle was no democrat, no supporter of mass participation; he viewed citizenship as appropriate for relatively few members of society. Further, he saw the practice of citizenship not as a solution to the problem of alienation but, rather, as a moral imperative, a natural law for man as political animal. Dagger appears to adopt this notion of citizenship as an ethical standard against which to judge the contemporary city. His specific analysis—that cities are too large, too fragmented, and characterized by too much residential mobility—is itself not very persuasive; the evidence he presents is impressionistic at best. But like Arkes, his general approach points us in the direction of a more satisfying normative theory of the city insofar as it invokes independently justified norms and seeks to apply them to the peculiar issues of urban politics.

In an obvious sense, the works we have just considered could not be more different. In the conventional left-right spectrum of American politics, Castells and Arkes are poles apart. For our purposes, however, their similarity in one respect is decisive, namely, their willingness to approach city politics in terms of political philosophy. Castells and Arkes address the urban crisis on the basis of general and abstract principles of judgment, in one case Marxist, in the other Kantian. Further, for each the problems of the city are to be regarded as distinctive, in one case involving the particular functional role of urban institutions in the structure of contemporary capitalism, in the other involving the special traits of social life in the modern city. Together they offer an exemplary basis from which we can begin to describe, in schematic terms, some of the requirements of a philosophy of urban politics.

Philosophy and Urban Politics

Let us begin with the assumption that we regard the city as a distinctive entity, and that we wish to view it as "political." That is, we wish to understand the city as a polity. Our task then would be to outline what we mean by a polity and to judge contemporary American cities in terms of that outline. We begin, that is, not from empirical reality but from a rational ideal which we then apply to the everyday facts of urban life.

Borrowing from classical traditions, let us postulate four characteristics which any entity must have if it is to fit with our general concept of the political. The first of these is *plurality*. Inherent in the notion of politics is the idea of confronting and resolving differences. Such differences might be cultural, material, or moral; in the end, they will likely manifest themselves as intellectual differences. In any case, some kind of serious and salient disagreement—a plurality of views—would seem to be necessary for politics. Indeed, if all of us agreed on all important things, then it is hard to imagine why we would even have such a notion as the "political." This is roughly an argument that Aristotle made against Plato in Book 2 of the *Politics*. It suggests that a completely hermetic unity, while perhaps attractive in some sense, would nonetheless violate the very concept of political life.

Beyond this politics also requires *equality*. This does not necessarily mean the strict leveling of incomes, though it might. It does not even mean the recognition and protection of equal opportunities, though again that is certainly possible. Rather, politics requires that the plurality of viewpoints essential to politics be regarded as a plurality of peers. Were this not the case, then plurality would be of no consequence. For example, if only one viewpoint among many were granted any real efficacy and voice, then plurality would be utterly hollow. In John Locke's formulation, the city would cease to be a polity and would become instead something of a family ruled by a patriarch in which the father's voice—or the king's voice—would be the only one heard. Locke's point is that political relations differ from family relations precisely because they involve disagreements among equals.[11] Further, our very concept of politics also requires that differences be worked out on their own terms rather than in terms of some preestablished and external principle of hierarchy. The winning view should be the one that is most persuasive, not the one articulated by some person arbitrarily placed in authority.

In view of this, the polity must also be *a moral entity*. Nothing very portentous is intended here. We need not conjure images of God, natural law, or other eternal verities. But there is a sense in which politics, concerned as it is with questions of right and wrong, must involve the kinds of discussion characteristic of moral discourse. Stated otherwise, our notion of politics would seem to require that political views be presented not merely as attitudes or opinions but as *arguments* to be defended or refuted. In the plurality of viewpoints described above, each gains its legitimacy, earns its "peerage," by presenting reasons in its behalf. Without such reasons, without a rational argument on its side, there would be no basis for taking it seriously; and it would seem to have no basis for attempting to impose itself on the rest. In this sense, politics is, at least in part, a conversation in which the discussants seek to discover the strongest arguments. This reliance on argument, on the determination to operate in terms of well-justified principles, is an essential property of moral discourse.

Finally, a polity must have *efficacy*. By this I do not quite mean what most political scientists mean, a feeling of power, a psychological state in which the individual is free from a sense of frustration and impotence. Rather, I refer to a kind of systemic power—the ability of a political system to see its judgments put into practice.[12] Politics is not only a conversation; it is also a process by which the fruits of conversation are given an empirical existence, in Hegelian terms, are embodied and made concrete. Our concept of politics requires that the polity be able to make laws, raise money, throw people in jail, build schools, mediate disputes, and the like. Without such a capacity all we have is a debating society. The ability to act in the world, to impose moral judgments upon the world in which we live, is a defining characteristic of politics.

This briefest sketch of the political can hardly satisfy us. I offer it largely for illustrative purposes. But assuming for the moment that it has some merit, what then are the implications for a philosophy of urban politics? What kind of agenda does it set for those of us who have normative concerns and who wish to go beyond the ideologies of urban politics?

I would identify three tasks. First is the job of specifying or fleshing out philosophical issues such as those raised by the outline above. For example, I have argued that equality is a necessary characteristic of a genuine polity. But of what does this equality consist? What kinds of specific equality conditions must exist if the requirements of political conversation are to be met? There is, of course, a huge philosophic literature on the concept of equality, and there is certainly no clear consensus on the subject. But it is in this literature that the philosopher of urban politics must look for clarification. In order to have a rational standard which we can bring to bear on issues of urban life, our concepts must be specified, their implications made clear, their adequacy defended. Thus for some, equality necessarily means equality of outcomes; only that can guarantee the possibility of true political conversation. But for others, equal opportunity would suffice; and for still others, treating equals equally and unequals unequally is really what we want. The philosopher of urbanism must get these issues clear, and must arrive at some specific and defended notion of equality, before he can begin to make empirical judgments. We would say much the same for the concepts of plurality, efficacy, and moral reasoning; our job is to clarify these notions insofar as they will provide standards for making empirical judgments regarding contemporary urban politics.

The making of such judgments is the second key task. Does the contemporary American city qualify as a "polity"? Again, the question cannot be answered unless we are clear in our minds about what a polity is, i.e., about what we take plurality, equality, moral discourse, and efficacy to be. But assuming that we have worked out such notions, at least provisionally, our job becomes one of examining the distinctive and peculiar characteristics of our cities to see if they pass muster. To my knowledge, there are few existing studies that would be of much help in completing such a task. Nonetheless, the following judgments can be suggested as illustrative empirical hypotheses.

1. *Plurality.* For sociological reasons alone, the American city seems to well satisfy the condition of plurality. Indeed, on some accounts this is precisely the political strength of urban areas. Racial and ethnic divisions, economic differences, geographic separations, cultural disagreements—such factors, which often appear to us destructive and vexing, nonetheless do assure that the city can be an arena for vital and active politics.[13]

2. *Equality.* The city fares much less well here. There is a great deal of evidence to suggest that certain viewpoints in urban politics are systematically "mobilized out" of the decisionmaking process, skewing the conversation and violating the principle of equality. Even many so-called pluralist studies admit as much. Indeed, in large part the debate over community power focused less on the degree of political inequality in the city than on its precise causes and consequences.[14]

3. *Moral discourse.* This appears to be the most difficult standard to apply; operationalizing the concept of moral discourse would be no easy task. Still, the "enterprise" image of the city-as-producer, along with a certain widespread reluctance to legislate morals, do suggest that the potential for moral discourse in urban America has not been adequately exploited. Indeed, this is a main theme of Arkes's book.

4. *Efficacy.* The American city is also importantly inefficacious. In part, this is a matter of law; according to Supreme Court doctrine, the municipal corporation is merely a child of the state, owing its existence and its power entirely to sovereign state entities. But also, the development of creative federalism, resulting in increasing federal leverage over localities, has served to circumscribe significantly the prerogatives of city governments. In general, we may say that the capacity of urban political systems to act independently—to legislate, to raise money, to allocate resources—is limited in some significant ways.

Again, these judgments are purely provisional and would be open to considerable dispute. Still, they illustrate the kinds of evaluative judgments urban political philosophers must make; they may, in the process, suggest a useful agenda for empirical research on the city.

The third task we face involves the practical application of such judgments. The philosopher of urban politics must search for ways of making the city more of a polity. This might involve any number of substantive and institutional recommendations, and would depend of course on the nature of the empirical judgments illustrated above. If, in fact, I am correct in saying that the city fails in terms of equality, moral discourse, and efficacy, then reform efforts should be focused in these areas. To be sure, the process by which one arrives at, and tests, suitable recommendations is by no means clear; but our approach at least has the virtue of identifying the kinds of recommendations to be sought and the kinds of problems to be resolved.

My own view is that the issue of equality is a serious one, but that it cannot be handled at the local level; political inequality is deeply rooted in national traditions and institutions which are, thus, the true sources of inequality in the city. Similarly, the problem of morality probably defies institutional remedies at any level; the propensity to operate in terms of moral categories cannot be created out of thin air. The problem of efficacy, on the other hand, might well be the subject of meaningful proposals with a distinctly urban focus. These could range from Constitutional arguments (a la Judge Cooley) in behalf of the implicit powers and prerogatives of municipal corporations, to the view that some cities should be granted statehood. Such proposals may or may not have intrinsic appeal. But they can be more soundly formulated, and more effectively defended, if developed in terms of specific, philosophically generated needs.

This particular theme—the problem of efficacy—may be worth pursuing a bit further. Despite the legal inferiority of the municipal corporation, we have always had—and still have—a strong tradition of local independence. From the heritage of the New England town, the antifederalist traditions of the Constitutional period, Tocqueville's powerful and urgent celebrations of local independence—from a variety of such sources we have retained the deep-seated idea that certain governmental functions are matters of local prerogative and that local governments are and ought to be fully able to take care of those functions.

This uneasy conflation of de jure inferiority and de facto independence is not of itself mischievous. In fact, it long provided the basis for a tacit and workable marriage of convenience between the forces of local control and those of administrative efficiency. However, events of the past two decades have served to undermine the balance of federal relations. In brief, the requirements, desires, and impulses of federal and state governments have been imposed as never before upon local jurisdictions. The mechanics of this are well known. The system of federal grants, by attaching strings to the transfer of large sums of money, has ensured that the composition of local budgets is significantly influenced by priorities established at the federal level. Similarly, the federal courts have dramatically increased the scope of federal law, thereby imposing a wide range of policy directives and requirements upon local decisionmakers. Court rulings pertaining to busing, police procedure, environmental quality, and housing policy are among numerous examples. Even the last apparent vestige of local control, zoning, is slowly but surely being eroded under the weight of judicial opinion.

The result is that local governments have increasingly become merely administrative entities rather than "political" entities as here defined. Their function, that is, has been more and more to administer public policies which are made at higher levels, to implement rather than decide. In saying this, I have no desire to revive the old distinction between politics and administration. I agree that administration is never the automatic, scientific, and neutral process it is sometimes thought to be; implementing policy itself involves decisions about who gets what, when, and why. But there is, nonetheless, a profound distinction between politics in the sense of collective deliberation and decisionmaking with reference to basic priorities, goals, and policies and the so-called politics of administration which is essentially discretionary, interstitial, and bureaucratic. The former is the activity of sovereign governments while the latter is the activity of administrative agencies. And urban governments in the United States have increasingly assumed this latter function, have become facilitating units carrying out the political will of some other political entity.

One problem here is that, despite all of this, urban governments are still expected to take care of themselves. While state and federal aid to cities currently constitutes a large proportion of municipal revenues, evidence strongly suggests that such contributions have not been commensurate with the additional burdens placed on local coffers. For example, in 1970 New York's Westchester County had to spend 47.6 percent of its *own* property tax revenues on programs mandated by the federal and state governments; by 1982, this already large figure had risen to 65.9 percent. The implication is that local governments are forced to function as administrative entities, yet are not supported as administrative agencies should be. They are expected to carry out someone else's policy, but to do it largely on their own.

Equally important, for our purposes, is the impact of such developments on the "efficacy" of urban governments. Revenues expended on federally mandated programs are revenues unavailable for supporting any number of locally generated policies. When this fact is coupled with the legal inferiority of the city, whereby the exercise of power is typically subject to legislative and judicial review at the state level, we can see the difficulties involved in sustaining city government as a political—i.e., deliberative and efficacious—entity.

In my judgment, questions of this kind are ultimately the proper focus of urban political philosophy. Just as the great theorists from Aristotle to Marx were concerned with practice as well as theory, so too must the philosopher of the city be willing to prescribe the concrete forms and policies of a more adequate urban politics. There are faint indications that we may soon have such a body of urban political thought. The very different writings of Castells and Arkes, whatever their merits, suggest a willingness to consider the unique potential of the city in terms of an explicit philosophical vision. Whether these authors and their critics will have any influence on the shape of urban politics remains to be seen. But in the absence of such efforts, we are likely to become less and less interested in the potentialities of city government. This would be unfortunate, because a good deal of what is important in

American politics in fact takes place in American cities.

I have claimed that American city politics is shaped by an ongoing conversation among three ideologies. There is a sense, though, in which this conversation is in fact less a dialogue than an obdurate confrontation. For since the underlying presuppositions of the ideologies typically remain unarticulated, the real issues between them are rarely raised. A philosophical approach to urban problems, on the other hand, offers the prospect of a true dialogue in which assumptions are explicit and open to analysis and evaluation. In this regard, the notion of the city as polity is particularly attractive. For such a city is not simply a construct of urban political philosophy, though it is that. It is also a setting which would conduce to the activity of urban political philosophy itself. That is, a city rich with a plurality of viewpoints, all equally participating in constructive discourse of a moral kind, would be a place in which the philosophical endeavor might naturally become an important and regular facet of the decisionmaking process.

But the connections are even deeper than this. For the very activity of philosophizing is itself a step toward the realization of the city as polity. While our effort to do justice to the agenda outlined above would not directly contribute to the equality or efficacy of the city, it might at least raise these issues for public consideration; further, such an effort would appear to constitute a tangible, if only preliminary, step toward the revitalization of moral discourse regarding urban problems.

Such remarks are not intended to paint an overly optimistic picture. The crisis of the cities, rooted in decades of social, economic, and political development, is not likely to collapse in the face of philosophical speculation. Nonetheless, all attempts to deal with urban problems are ultimately rooted in idea systems of one kind or another. To the degree that these systems are congenial to serious and meaningful dialogue regarding the most basic questions, we will be that much closer to a sensible and responsible approach to the urban crisis. Political philosophy can provide urbanists with a set of animating principles and with a constructive vision of a possible future against which to judge current practices and policies. As such, it is an absolutely essential tool for urbanists interested in improving the public lives of those who live and work in our cities.

NOTES
Chapter 1

1. Robert Dahl, "The Behavioral Approach in Political Science: Epitaph for a Monument to a Successful Protest," *American Political Science Review* 55 (December 1961).
2. On the "death" of political philosophy, see Peter Laslett's "Introduction" to his *Philosophy, Politics, and Society* (Oxford: Basil Blackwell, 1956).
3. See W. G. Runciman, *Social Science and Political Theory* (Cambridge: Cambridge University Press, 1969). For at least one attempt to bridge the normative-behavioral gap, see Dennis Thompson, *The Democratic Citizen* (Cambridge: Cambridge University Press, 1970).
4. Laurence J. R. Herson, "The Lost World of Municipal Government," *American Political Science Review* 51 (June 1957).
5. Charles R. Adrian, *Governing Urban America* (New York: McGraw-Hill, 1955).
6. For a summary, see Edward Banfield and James Q. Wilson, *City Politics* (New York: Random House, 1966), pp. 224-242.
7. For example, Edward Banfield, *Political Influence* (New York: Free Press, 1961). Here and above, I ignore the much earlier work of Charles Merriam and Harold Gosnell.
8. Robert Dahl, *Who Governs?* (New Haven: Yale University Press, 1961). Also, Nelson Polsby, *Community Power and Political Theory* 2nd ed. (New Haven: Yale University Press, 1980); Peter Bachrach and Morton Baratz, *Power and Poverty* (New York: Oxford University Press, 1970); M. Kent Jennings, *Community Influentials: The Elites of Atlanta* (New York: Macmillan, 1964); G. William Domhoff, *Who Really Rules?* (Santa Monica, Calif.: Goodyear, 1978); and Clarence Stone, "Systemic Power in Community Decision Making," *American Political Science Review* 74 (December 1980).
9. See, for example, Claude Fischer, "The City and Political Psychology," *American Political Science Review* 69 (June 1975).
10. The literature is well summarized by Brett Hawkins, *Politics and Urban Policies* (Indianapolis: Bobbs-Merrill, 1971).
11. See, for example, Oliver Williams, *Metropolitan Political Analysis* (New York: Free Press, 1971).
12. This is a premise of Banfield, *Political Influence*, pp. 307ff.
13. John Gunnell, "Deduction, Explanation and Social Scientific Inquiry," *American Political Science Review* 63 (December 1969); Richard Bernstein, *The Restructuring of Social and Political Theory* (Philadelphia: University of Pennsylvania Press, 1976); Eugene F. Miller, "Positivism, Historicism, and Political Inquiry," *American Political Science Review* 66 (September 1972); Peter J. Steinberger, "Hegel as a Social Scientist," *American Political Science Review* 71 (March 1977).

14. Peter Achinstein, *Concepts of Science* (Baltimore: Johns Hopkins University Press, 1968), pp. 92ff.
15. Stephen Toulmin, *The Philosophy of Science* (New York: Harper & Row, 1963).
16. Charles McCoy and John Playford, eds., *Apolitical Politics* (New York: Crowell, 1967).
17. Dahl, *Who Governs?*
18. Jewel Bellush and Stephen David, *Race and Politics in New York City* (New York: Praeger, 1971).
19. Ibid.
20. P. H. Partridge, "Politics, Philosophy, Ideology," in Anthony Quinton, ed., *Political Philosophy* (Oxford: Oxford University Press, 1967).
21. Ibid., p. 33.
22. Ibid., p. 34.
23. Nannerl O. Keohane, "Philosophy, Theory, Ideology," *Political Theory* 4 (February 1976).
24. Ibid., p. 82.
25. Ibid., p. 85.
26. Ibid., p. 83.
27. Leo Strauss, "What Is Political Philosophy?" *Journal of Politics* 18 (August 1957); John Plamenatz, "The Use of Political Theory," *Political Studies* 77 (1960).
28. See Willard Mullins, "On the Concept of Ideology in Political Science," *American Political Science Review* 66 (June 1972); Edward Shils, "The Concept and Function of Ideology," *International Encyclopedia of the Social Sciences*, Vol. 7, pp. 66–76; Neil Smelser, *The Theory of Collective Behavior* (New York: Free Press, 1962); Karl Mannheim, *Ideology and Utopia* (New York: Harcourt, Brace & World, n.d.); George Lichtheim, *The Concept of Ideology* (New York: Random House, 1967).
29. Quentin Skinner, "History and Ideology in the English Revolution," *Historical Journal* 8 (1965).
30. Quentin Skinner, *The Foundations of Modern Political Thought* Vols. 1 and 2 (Cambridge: Cambridge University Press, 1978).
31. See Thomas P. Jenkin, *The Study of Political Theory* (Garden City, N.Y.: Doubleday, 1955); Anthony Quinton, *Political Philosophy* (Oxford: Oxford University Press, 1967); S. I. Benn and R. S. Peters, *Social Principles and the Democratic State* (London: Allen & Unwin, 1959).
32. For a good introduction see Robert Paul Wolff, *In Defense of Anarchism* (New York: Harper & Row, 1967).
33. Stephen Salkever, "Virtue, Obligation and Politics," *American Political Science Review* 68 (March 1974).
34. A. P. D'Entreves, *The Medieval Contribution to Political Thought* (Oxford: Oxford University Press, 1939).

35. For a good discussion, see John Dewey, *The Public and Its Problems* (Chicago: Swallow Press, n.d.).
36. Of course, I am here distinguishing Plato's systematic writings on politics from his reports of the conversations of Socrates. The *Crito* is obviously and explicitly concerned with the issue of political obligation.
37. Keith Brown, ed., *Hobbes Studies* (Cambridge: Harvard University Press, 1965).
38. See Michael Oakeshott, *On Human Conduct* (Oxford: Oxford University Press, 1975), pp. 108ff.

Chapter 2

1. For some general treatments, see Edward Banfield and James Q. Wilson, *City Politics* (New York: Random House, 1966); Richard S. Childs, *Civic Victories* (New York: Harper, 1952); and Harold Stone, Don Price, and Kathryn Stone, *City Manager Government in the United States* (Chicago: Social Science Research Council, 1940).
2. See, for example, Richard Hofstadter, *The Age of Reform* (New York: Random House, n.d.)
3. Charles Adrian and Charles Press, *Governing Urban America* (New York: McGraw-Hill, 1972), p.226. According to the *Municipal Yearbook*, as of 1980 these figures were largely unchanged.
4. Ibid., p. 49.
5. For a general treatment of the role of planning in American politics, see Grant McConnell, *Private Power and American Democracy* (New York: Random House, 1970).
6. See Andreas Faludi, *A Reader in Planning Theory* (Oxford: Pergamon Press, 1973), p. 41; Ruth Glass, "The Evaluation of Planning: Some Sociological Considerations," *International Social Science Journal* ll (1959); Melvin Webber, "Comprehensive Planning and Social Responsibility: Toward an AIP Consensus on the Profession's Roles and Purposes," *Journal of the American Institute of Planners* 29 (November 1963); John Friedmann, "A Response to Altshuler: Comprehensive Planning as a Process," *Journal of the American Institute of Planners* (August 1965).
7. Adrian and Press, *Governing Urban America*, p. 491.
8. See Murray Schiesel, *The Politics of Efficiency* (Berkeley: University of California Press, 1977), pp. 1–25.
9. See Vernon L. Parrington, *Main Currents in American Thought (Vol. 1)* (New York: Harcourt, Brace World, 1954), p. 18.
10. For general treatments, see Perry Miller, *American Puritans* (New York: Peter Smith, 1959); and Michael Walzer, *The Revolution of the Saints* (Cambridge: Harvard University Press, 1965).
11. Hofstadter, *Age of Reform*, p. 131.

12. Ibid., p. 140.

13. Ibid., p. 168. For an important clarification of Hofstadter's general approach, see John Buenker, *Urban Liberalism and Progressive Reform* (New York: Norton, 1978).

14. Edward Banfield and James Q. Wilson, "Public Regardingness as a Value Premise in Voting Behavior," *American Political Science Review* 58 (December 1964).

15. See Raymond Wolfinger and J.O. Field, "Political Ethos and the Structure of City Government," *American Political Science Review* 60 (June 1966).

16. For a summary of the relevant literature, see Brett Hawkins, *Politics and Urban Policies* (Indianapolis: Bobbs-Merrill, 1971).

17. See pp. 37-40 below.

18. Max Weber, "Bureaucracy," in *From Max Weber*, ed. by Hans Gerth and C. W. Mills (New York: Oxford University Press, 1958), pp. 196-244.

19. Karl Popper, *The Open Society and Its Enemies (Vol. 1)* (Princeton: Princeton University Press, 1966), pp. 158-160.

20. See Oliver Williams, *Metropolitan Political Analysis* (New York: Free Press, 1971).

21. Faludi, *Reader in Planning Theory*, p. 41.

22. Webber, "Comprehensive Planning," p. 232.

23. Ibid., p. 236. See also Glass, "Evaluation of Planning," p. 45; and Friedmann, "Response to Altshuler," p. 195.

24. For a classic statement of the distinction between politics and administration, see Frank Goodnow, *Politics and Administration* (New York: Russell & Russell, 1900).

25. Robert Caro, *The Power Broker* (New York: Random House, 1974).

26. Chester Hartman, et al., *Yerba Buena* (San Francisco: Glide Publications, 1974).

27. Ibid., p. 45.

28. Ibid., p. 51.

29. Ronald O. Loveridge, *City Managers in Legislative Politics* (Indianapolis: Bobbs-Merrill, 1971); Michael Vasu, *Politics and Planning* (Chapel Hill: University of North Carolina Press, 1979).

30. Alan Altshuler, *The City Planning Process* (Ithaca: Cornell University Press, 1966).

31. Robert Goodman, *After the Planners* (New York: Touchstone Press, 1973).

32. Carl Becker, *The Heavenly City of the Eighteenth Century Philosophers* (New Haven: Yale University Press, 1932), p. 60. See also Peter Gay, *The Enlightenment: An Interpretation* (New York: Random House, 1966), pp. 11-14; Claude Helvetius, *A Treatise on Man (Vol. 1)* (London: Albion

Press, 1810), p. 93n; Marquis de Condorcet, *Selected Writings*, ed. by K. M. Baker (Indianapolis: Bobbs-Merrill, 1976); Henri de St.-Simon, *Social Organization, The Science of Man, and Other Writings* (New York: Harper & Row, 1964), pp. 13, 17.

33. Becker, *Heavenly City*, p. 60.
34. Condorcet, *Selected Writings*, p. 93. See also pp. 5, 15, 20-21; and Helvetius, *Treatise on Man (Vol. 1)*, pp. 94, 228-233; Denis Diderot, *The Encyclopedia: Selections* (Indianapolis: Bobbs-Merrill, 1965), especially essays by D'Alembert ("Preliminary Discourse"), Diderot ("Eclecticism"), and an anonymous essay entitled "Observation"; Auguste Comte, *A General View of Positivism* (London: George Routledge & Sons, 1908), pp. 3, 34-41, 59; Auguste Comte, *The Positive Philosophy of Auguste Comte (Vol. 2)* (London: Kegan Paul, 1893), pp. 35-36, 62-63, 79-92, 101-104, 413; St.-Simon, *Social Organization* . . ., pp. 13-21, 23-27; and Karl Mannheim, *Man and Society in an Age of Reconstruction* (New York: Harcourt, 1944), pp. 43, 93, 152, 240, 258-266.
35. Faludi, *Reader in Planning Theory*, p. 1.
36. Preston LeBreton and Dale Henning, *Planning Theory* (Englewood Cliffs, N. J.: Prentice-Hall, 1961), p. 85.
37. Webber, "Comprehensive Planning," p. 233; also pp. 236 and 240.
38. Richard E. Klosterman, "Foundations for Normative Planning," *Journal of the American Institute of Planners* (January 1978).
39. See Paul Davidoff, "Advocacy and Pluralism in Planning," *Journal of the American Institute of Planners*, Vol. 31 (November 1965).
40. See Goodman, *After the Planners*.
41. Condorcet, *Selected Writings*, p. 5.
42. Ibid., p. 6.
43. Ibid., p. 12.
44. Ibid., p. 23.
45. Ibid., p. 211-218, 255-264.
46. See Comte, *General View of Positivism*, pp. 58-62, 78-80, 116-121; Comte, *Positive Philosophy*, pp. 72-74; St.-Simon, *Social Organization*. . ., pp. 21-22, 27; and Mannheim, *Man and Society*, pp. 244-249, 262.
47. Webber, "Comprehensive Planning," p. 237.
48. Ibid., p. 236-237.
49. Ibid., p. 239. See also LeBreton and Henning, *Planning Theory*, p. 343; and Faludi, *Reader in Planning Theory*, p. 113.
50. Immanuel Kant, *Prolegomena to Any Future Metaphysics* (Indianapolis: Bobbs-Merrill, 1950).
51. G. W. F. Hegel, *The Philosophy of History* (New York: Dover, 1956).
52. See Karl Marx, *The German Ideology* (New York: International Publishers, 1970); Karl Mannheim, *Ideology and Utopia* (New York: Harcourt, Brace & World, n.d.); and George Lichtheim, *The Concept of Ideology* (New York: Random House, 1967).

53. See Wilhelm Dilthey, *Pattern and Meaning in History* (New York: Harper & Row, 1962); Alfred Schutz, *The Phenomenology of the Social World* (Evanston, Ill.: Northwestern University Press, 1967); Peter Berger and Thomas Luckmann, *The Social Construction of Reality* (Garden City, N. Y.: Doubleday, 1967); John Gunnell, "Deduction, Explanation, and Social Scientific Inquiry," *American Political Science Review* 63 (December 1969); Eugene F. Miller, "Positivism, Historicism, and Political Inquiry," *American Political Science Review* 66 (September 1972); Richard Bernstein, *The Restructuring of Social and Political Theory* (Philadelphia: University of Pennsylvania Press, 1976).
54. See Thomas Kuhn, *The Structure of Scientific Revolutions* (Chicago: University of Chicago Press, 1970); and Paul K. Feyerabend, *Against Method* (Atlantic Highlands, N. J.: Humanities Press, 1975).
55. Jean-Jacques Rousseau, "A Discourse on the Arts and Sciences," in *The Social Contract and Discourses*, ed. by G. D. H. Cole (New York: E. P. Dutton, 1950), p. 243.
56. Georges Sorel, *The Illusions of Progress*, ed. by John Stanley (Berkeley: University of California Press, 1969); and Michael Oakeshott, *Rationalism in Politics* (London: Methuen, 1981).
57. See Arnold Brecht, *Political Theory* (Princeton: Princeton University Press, 1959); and Heinz Eulau, ed., *Behavioralism in Political Science* (New York: Atherton, 1969).
58. Helvetius, *Treatise on Man (Vol. 1)*, p. 207.
59. David Hume, *A Treatise on Human Nature* (Oxford: Clarendon Press, 1888), p. 415. See also Helvetius, *Treatise on Man (Vol. 2)* p. 317; Comte, *General View of Positivism*, pp. 18-21, 98-100, 109-111; and Mannheim, *Man and Society*, pp. 67ff.
60. George Sabine, *A History of Political Thought* (Hinsdale, Ill.: Dryden Press, 1973), p. 555. Sabine's treatment is superficial, as befits a textbook, but this passage is particularly apt. For a deeper and much more satisfying account, see Stephen G. Salkever, " 'Cool Reflexion' and the Criticism of Values: Is, Ought, and Objectivity in Hume's Social Science," *American Political Science Review* 74 (March 1980).
61. Helvetius, *Treatise on Man (Vol. 2)*, p. 317; also *Vol. 1*, pp. 124-133 and *Vol. 2*, pp.342-360. Also, Comte, *General View of Positivism*, pp. 14-21; and Jeremy Bentham, *The Principles of Morals and Legislation* (New York: Hafner, 1948), pp. 1-8, 70.
62. Faludi, *Reader in Planning Theory*, p. 20.
63. Ibid., p. 23.
64. Ibid., p. 32.
65. Ibid., p. 33-36.
66. Weber, " 'Objectivity' in the Social Sciences and Social Policy," in E. Shils and H. Finch, eds., *Max Weber on the Methodology of the Social Sciences* (Glencoe, Ill.: Free Press, 1949).

67. Charles Taylor, "Neutrality in Political Science," in Peter Laslett and W. G. Runciman eds., *Philosophy, Politics and Society* (3rd Series) (Oxford: Basil Blackwell, 1969).
68. George Lukács, *History and Class Consciousness* (Cambridge: MIT Press, 1971); Max Horkheimer, *Critical Theory* (New York: Seabury Press, 1972); Herbert Marcuse, *One-Dimensional Man* (Boston: Beacon Press, 1964); Jürgen Habermas, *Knowledge and Human Interests* (Boston: Beacon Press, 1971).
69. Immanuel Kant, *Foundations of the Metaphysics of Morals* (Indianapolis: Bobbs-Merrill, 1959).
70. William Frankena, *Ethics* (Englewood Cliffs, N. J.: Prentice-Hall, 1963).
71. Donald Michael "Urban Policy in the Nationalized Society," *Journal of the American Institute of Planners* (November 1965). See also by Michael, *The Unprepared Society* (New York: Basic Books, 1968).
72. Michael, "Urban Policy," p. 283.
73. Ibid., p. 286. This view is tempered somewhat in *Unprepared Society*, p. 10.
74. Ibid., p. 287; *Unprepared Society*, pp. 78-79.
75. Idem.
76. Idem.
77. Ibid., p. 286; *Unprepared Society*, pp. 51-56. See also Jeremy Bentham, *A Fragment on Government* (Oxford: Clarendon Press, 1891), pp. 216-228; Bentham, *Principles of Morals and Legislation*, p. 63; Mannheim, *Man and Society*, pp. 267-273, 336; Helvetius, *Treatise on Man (Vol. 2)*, pp. 180-184, 317-320; Comte, *General View of Positivism*, pp. 101-104, 127-132; Comte, *Positive Philosophy*, pp. 75-77; St.-Simon, *Social Organization*, pp. 72-79.
78. Michael, "Urban Policy," p. 287. See also Glass, "Evaluation of Planning," p. 63; Webber, "Comprehensive Planning," pp. 238-239.
79. See Richard Flathman, *Political Obligation* (New York: Atheneum, 1972).
80. Blair Campbell, "Helvetius and the Roots of the Closed Society," *American Political Science Review* 68 (March 1974).
81. In my judgment, Wolin in fact includes many writers in this group who do not really belong.
82. Sheldon Wolin, *Politics and Vision* (Boston: Little, Brown, 1960), pp. 360-361.
83. Ibid., p. 364-365.
84. Robert Nisbet, *The Quest for Community* (Oxford: Oxford University Press, 1953).
85. Alexis de Tocqueville, *Democracy in America (Vol. 1)* (New York: Random House, 1945), pp. 62-71.
86. Ibid. *(Vol. 2)*, p. 336.

Chapter 3

1. Peter Marris and Martin Rein, *Dilemmas of Social Reform* (New York: Atherton Press, 1967).
2. See Daniel Patrick Moynihan, *Maximum Feasible Misunderstanding* (New York: Free Press, 1969).
3. For a general discussion see Robert Dahl, *A Preface to Democratic Theory* (New Haven: Yale University Press, 1963).
4. See Peter Bachrach, *The Theory of Democratic Elitism* (Boston: Little, Brown, 1967).
5. Alexis de Tocqueville, *Democracy in America (Vol. 1)* (New York: Random House, 1945), p. 67.
6. Ibid., p. 62.
7. Ibid., p. 63.
8. Ibid., p. 70.
9. Ibid., p. 64.
10. Ibid., p. 69.
11. Quoted in Anwar Syed, *The Political Theory of American Local Government* (New York: Random House, 1966), p. 54.
12. Ibid., p. 55.
13. Ibid., p. 61.
14. Douglas Yates, *Neighborhood Democracy* (Lexington, Mass.: D. C. Heath, 1973), p. 18; and Morton and Lucia White, *The Intellectual versus the City* (Toronto: New American Library, 1964), pp. 150–158.
15. Joseph Kershaw, *Government against Poverty* (Chicago: Markham, 1970), pp. 50–71.
16. Yates, *Neighborhood Democracy*, pp. 28–30. See also Harry C. Boyte, *The Backyard Revolution* (Philadelphia: Temple University Press, 1980).
17. Stokely Carmichael and Charles V. Hamilton, *Black Power* (New York: Random House, 1967).
18. Ibid., p. 167.
19. Ibid., p. 172.
20. Ibid., pp. 172–173.
21. Ibid., p. 176.
22. Milton Kotler, *Neighborhood Government* (New York: Bobbs-Merrill, 1969).
23. Ibid., p. 11.
24. Ibid., p. 2.
25. Ibid., pp. 98–100.
26. Alan Altshuler, *Community Control* (New York: Bobbs-Merrill, 1970).
27. Charles Hampden-Turner, *From Poverty to Dignity* (New York: Doubleday, 1974). See also Karl Hess, *Community Technology* (New York: Harper & Row, 1979).

28. Ibid., p. 125.
29. Ibid., p. 156.
30. See Joseph Zimmerman, *The Federated City* (New York: St. Martin's, 1972); George Fredrickson, ed., *Neighborhood Control in the 1970's* (New York: Chandler, 1973), pp. 263-266; David Morris and Karl Hess, *Neighborhood Power* (Boston: Beacon Press, 1975), pp. 100-101; and Boyte, *Backyard Revolution*, pp. 44ff.
31. Eric Nordlinger, *Decentralizing the City* (Boston: Boston Urban Observatory, 1972).
32. Altshuler, *Community Control*, p. 44.
33. Robert Nisbet, *The Quest for Community* (Oxford: Oxford University Press, 1953).
34. Altshuler, *Community Control*, pp. 19-34.
35. Irving Kristol, "Decentralization for What?" *The Public Interest* (Spring 1968).
36. Altshuler, *Community Control*, pp. 37-44.
37. For relevant studies, see Ralph Kramer, *Participation of the Poor* (Englewood Cliffs, N. J.: Prentice-Hall, 1969); Yates, *Neighborhood Democracy*; Kershaw, *Government against Poverty*; and J. David Greenstone and Paul Peterson, *Race and Authority in Urban Politics* (Chicago: University of Chicago Press, 1976).
38. On the distinction between "positive" and "negative" liberty, see Isaiah Berlin, *Four Essays on Liberty* (Oxford: Oxford University Press, 1968).
39. For very different but related perspectives along these lines, see John Dewey, *The Public and Its Problems* (Chicago: Swallow Press, n.d.); Michael Oakeshott, *On Human Conduct* (Oxford: Oxford University Press, 1975); and Hannah Arendt, *The Human Condition* (Chicago: University of Chicago Press, 1969).
40. Dewey, *The Public and Its Problems*, pp. 22-23.
41. To call Rousseau the first great communalist is not to deny the importance of certain premodern political philosophers—from Plato to Althusius—in the development of the notion of community. The communalist ideology discussed here, however, is a distinctly modern conception, with its notions of participation, self-determination, and moral relativism and its almost existential belief in the silence of the universe. Thus, while the debt to the classics is certainly acknowledged, Rousseau remains a fitting starting point for the discussion of the philosophic bases of contemporary communalism.
42. Jean-Jacques Rousseau, *The Social Contract and Discourses*, ed. by G. D. H. Cole (New York: E. P. Dutton, 1950).
43. For a good recent treatment, see Arthur Melzer, "Rousseau and the Problem of Bourgeois Society," *American Political Science Review* 74 (December 1980).

44. Karl Marx, *Early Writings*, ed. by T. B. Bottomore (New York: McGraw-Hill, 1963).
45. Ibid., pp. 125–129.
46. Ibid., pp. 155–162.
47. Hampden-Turner, *From Poverty to Dignity*, p. 7.
48. Ibid., p. 14.
49. Ibid., p. 17.
50. Carmichael and Hamilton, *Black Power*, pp. 37–44.
51. Kotler, *Neighborhood Government*, pp. 39, 98. See also Hess, *Community Technology*, pp. 29ff.
52. Morris and Hess, *Neighborhood Power*, pp. 104–105. See also Boyte, *Backyard Revolution*, pp. 167ff.
53. Hampden-Turner, *From Poverty to Dignity*, p. 154.
54. Ibid., p. 137.
55. Ibid., p. 156.
56. For example, see Robert Bish and Vincent Ostrom, *Understanding Urban Government* (Washington, D. C.: American Enterprise Institute, 1973), pp. 95–96.
57. On the political relevance of autonomy, see Robert Paul Wolff, *In Defense of Anarchism* (New York: Harper & Row, 1976).
58. Rousseau, *Social Contract*, pp. 18–19.
59. Bachrach, *Theory of Democratic Elitism*.
60. See also Carole Pateman, *The Problem of Political Obligation* (New York: Wiley, 1979).
61. On the origins of "civic humanism," see J. G. A. Pocock, *The Machiavellian Moment* (Princeton: Princeton University Press, 1975).

Chapter 4

1. Robert Nozick, *Anarchy, State, and Utopia* (New York: Basic Books, 1974), pp. 18–19.
2. Jean-Jacques Rousseau, *The Social Contract and Discourses*, ed. by G. D. H. Cole (New York: E. P. Dutton, 1950), p. 26.
3. Alexander Hamilton, James Madison, and John Jay, *The Federalist Papers* (New York: New American Library, 1961).
4. Ibid., p. 79.
5. Ibid., p. 81.
6. Ibid., p. 78.
7. Ibid., p. 79.
8. Ibid., pp. 80–83.
9. Daniel Patrick Moynihan, *Maximum Feasible Misunderstanding* (New York: Free Press, 1969).
10. Edward Banfield, *The Unheavenly City Revisited* (Boston: Little, Brown, 1971).

11. Ibid., p. 53.
12. Ibid., pp. 61-62.
13. Ibid., pp. 3-10.
14. Oscar Lewis, *Tepoztlan: Village in Mexico* (New York: Holt, 1960).
15. Banfield, *Unheavenly City Revisited*, pp. 78-84.
16. Ibid., p. 263.
17. Ibid., p. 271.
18. Ibid., p. 273.
19. Robert Bish and Vincent Ostrom, *Understanding Urban Government* (Washington, D.C.: American Enterprise Institute, 1973).
20. Ibid., pp. 39-41.
21. Ibid., pp. 46-48.
22. Ibid., pp. 95-99.
23. C. B. Macpherson, *The Political Theory of Possessive Individualism* (Oxford: Oxford University Press, 1962).
24. Thomas Hobbes, *Leviathan* (Parts 1 and 2) (New York: Bobbs-Merrill, 1958).
25. Ibid., pp. 51-60.
26. Aristotle, *The Politics*, ed. by E. Barker (Oxford: Oxford University Press, 1976), pp. 280-281.
27. Rousseau, "A Discourse on the Origin of Inequality," in *The Social Contract and Discourses*.
28. G. W. F. Hegel, *The Philosophy of History* (New York: Dover, 1956).
29. Nozick, *Anarchy, State, Utopia*, pp. 10-18.
30. Hobbes, *Leviathan*, pp. 104-110.
31. Ibid., p. 49.
32. John Locke, *The Second Treatise of Government* (New York: Library of Liberal Arts, 1956), p. 5.
33. Ibid., p. 6.
34. Isaiah Berlin, *Four Essays on Liberty* (Oxford: Oxford University Press, 1968).
35. Milton Friedman, *Capitalism and Freedom* (Chicago: University of Chicago Press, 1962).

Chapter 5

1. Alan Lupo, Frank Colcord, and Edmund Fowler, *Rites of Way: The Politics of Transportation in Boston and the U.S. City* (Boston: Little, Brown, 1971).
2. Emmett Buell, *School Desegregation and Defended Neighborhoods* (Lexington, Mass.: Lexington Books, 1982).
3. Peter J. Steinberger, "Social Context and Political Efficacy," *Sociology and Social Research* 65 (January 1981), pp. 129-141; Peter J. Steinberger, "Political Participation and Communality: A Cultural/In-

terpersonal Approach," *Rural Sociology* 46 (Spring 1981), pp. 7-19; and Peter J. Steinberger, "Urban Politics and Communality," *Urban Affairs Quarterly* 20 (Summer 1984). For a more general treatment, see Michael P. Smith, *The City and Social Theory* (New York: St. Martin's, Press 1979).

4. See, for example, Paul Peterson, *City Limits* (Chicago: University of Chicago Press, 1981), pp. 218-219.

5. Manuel Castells, *The Urban Question* (Cambridge, Mass.: MIT Press, 1977). See also William K. Tabb and Larry Sawers, eds., *Marxism and the Metropolis* (New York: Oxford University Press, 1978); David Harvey, *Social Justice and the City* (Baltimore: Johns Hopkins University Press, 1973); Michael Dear and Allen J. Scott, eds., *Urbanization and Urban Planning in Capitalist Society* (New York: Methuen, 1981); Pierre Clavel, John Forester, and William W. Goldsmith, eds., *Urban Regional Planning in an Age of Austerity* (New York: Pergamon Press, 1980); Ira Katznelson, *City Trenches* (Chicago: University of Chicago Press, 1981); and Smith, *The City and Social Theory*.

6. Castells, *Urban Question*, pp. 125ff.

7. John H. Mollenkopf, "The Postwar Politics of Urban Development," in Tabb and Sawers, *Marxism and the Metropolis*, pp. 117-151.

8. Richard Child Hill, "Fiscal Collapse and Political Struggle in Decaying Central Cities in the United States," in Tabb and Sawers, *Marxism and the Metropolis*, pp. 213-240.

9. Hadley Arkes, *The Philosopher in the City* (Princeton: Princeton University Press, 1981).

10. Richard Dagger, "Metropolis, Memory, and Citizenship," *American Journal of Political Science* 25 (November 1981).

11. John Locke, *The Second Treatise of Government* (New York: Library of the Liberal Arts, 1956), Chapter 6.

12. Hannah Arendt, *On Violence* (New York: Harcourt, Brace & World, 1970), pp. 44ff.

13. This theme of plurality has been pursued most vigorously in the various writings of Jane Jacobs.

14. See Peter Bachrach and Morton Baratz, *Power and Poverty* (New York: Oxford University Press, 1970).

REFERENCES

Achinstein, Peter, *Concepts of Science* (Baltimore: Johns Hopkins University Press, 1968).
Adrian, Charles R., *Governing Urban America* (New York: McGraw-Hill, 1955).
Alinsky, Saul, *Reveille for Radicals* (New York: Random House, 1969).
Altshuler, Alan, *The City Planning Process* (Ithaca: Cornell University Press, 1966).
Altshuler, Alan, *Community Control* (New York: Bobbs-Merrill, 1970).
Arendt, Hannah, *The Human Condition* (Chicago: University of Chicago Press, 1969).
Arendt, Hannah, *On Violence* (New York: Harcourt, Brace & World, 1970).
Aristotle, *Politics*, ed. by E. Barker (Oxford: Oxford University Press, 1976).
Arkes, Hadley, *The Philosopher in the City* (Princeton: Princeton University Press, 1981).
Bachrach, Peter, *The Theory of Democratic Elitism* (Boston: Little, Brown, 1967).
Bachrach, Peter and Morton Baratz, *Power and Poverty* (New York: Oxford University Press, 1970).
Banfield, Edward, *Political Influence* (New York: Free Press, 1961).
Banfield, Edward, *The Unheavenly City Revisited* (Boston: Little, Brown, 1971).
Banfield, Edward and James Q. Wilson, "Public Regardingness as a Value Premise in Voting Behavior," *American Political Science Review* 58 (December 1964).
Banfield, Edward and James Q. Wilson, *City Politics* (New York: Random House, 1966).
Becker, Carl, *The Heavenly City of the Eighteenth Century Philosophers* (New Haven: Yale University Press, 1932).
Bellush, Jewel and Stephen David, *Race and Politics in New York City* (New York: Praeger, 1971).
Benn, S. I. and R. S. Peters, *Social Principles and the Democratic State* (London: Allen & Unwin, 1959).

Bentham, Jeremy, *A Fragment on Government* (Oxford: Clarendon Press, 1891).

Bentham, Jeremy, *The Principles of Morals and Legislation* (New York: Hafner, 1948).

Berger, Peter and Thomas Luckmann, *The Social Construction of Reality* (Garden City, N.Y.: Doubleday, 1967).

Berlin, Isaiah, *Four Essays on Liberty* (Oxford: Oxford University Press, 1968).

Bernstein, Richard, *The Restructuring of Social and Political Theory* (Philadelphia: University of Pennsylvania Press, 1976).

Bish, Robert and Vincent Ostrom, *Understanding Urban Government* (Washington: American Enterprise Institute, 1973).

Boyte, Harry C., *The Backyard Revolution* (Philadelphia: Temple University Press, 1980).

Brecht, Arnold, *Political Theory* (Princeton: Princeton University Press, 1959).

Brown, Keith, ed., *Hobbes Studies* (Cambridge: Harvard University Press, 1965).

Buell, Emmett, *School Desegregation and Defended Neighborhoods* (Lexington, Mass.: Lexington Books, 1982).

Buenker, John, *Urban Liberalism and Progressive Reform* (New York: Norton, 1978).

Campbell, Blair, "Helvetius and the Roots of the Closed Society," *American Political Science Review* 68 (March 1974).

Carmichael, Stokely and Charles V. Hamilton, *Black Power* (New York: Random House, 1967).

Caro, Robert, *The Power Broker* (New York: Random House, 1974).

Castells, Manuel, *The Urban Question* (Cambridge, Mass.: M I T Press, 1977).

Childs, Richard S., *Civic Victories* (New York: Harper, 1952).

Clavel, Pierre, John Forester, and William W. Goldsmith, eds., *Urban Regional Planning in an Age of Austerity* (New York: Pergamon Press, 1980).

Comte, Auguste, *The Positive Philosophy of Auguste Comte*, 2 vols. (London: Kegan Paul, 1893).

Comte, Auguste, *A General View of Positivism* (London: George Routledge & Sons, 1908).

Condorcet, Marquis de, *Selected Writings*, ed. by K. M. Baker (Indianapolis: Bobbs-Merrill, 1976).

Dagger, Richard, "Metropolis, Memory, and Citizenship," *American Journal of Political Science* 25 (November 1981).

Dahl, Robert, "The Behavioral Approach in Political Science: Epitaph for a Monument to a Successful Protest," *American Political Science*

Review 55 (December 1961).

Dahl, Robert, *Who Governs?* (New Haven: Yale University Press, 1961).

Dahl, Robert, *A Preface to Democratic Theory* (New Haven: Yale University Press, 1963).

Davidoff, Paul, "Advocacy and Pluralism in Planning," *Journal of the American Institute of Planners* 31 (November 1965).

Davidoff, Paul and Thomas A. Reiner, "A Choice Theory of Planning," *Journal of the American Institute of Planners* 28 (May 1962).

Dear, Michael and Allen J. Scott, eds., *Urbanization and Urban Planning in Capitalist Society* (New York: Methuen, 1981).

D'Entreves, A. P., *The Medieval Contribution to Political Thought* (Oxford: Oxford University Press, 1939).

de Tocqueville, Alexis, *Democracy in America*, 2 vols. (New York: Random House, 1945).

Dewey, John, *The Public and Its Problems* (Chicago: Swallow Press, no date).

Diderot, Denis, *The Encyclopedia: Selections* (Indianapolis: Bobbs-Merrill, 1965).

Dilthey, Wilhelm, *Pattern and Meaning in History* (New York: Harper & Row, 1962).

Domhoff, William, *Who Really Rules?* (Santa Monica, Calif.: Goodyear, 1978).

Eulau, Heinz, ed., *Behavioralism in Political Science* (New York: Atherton, 1969).

Faludi, Andreas, ed., *A Reader in Planning Theory* (Oxford: Pergamon Press, 1973).

Feyerabend, Paul K., *Against Method* (Atlantic Highlands, N. J.: Humanities Press, 1975).

Fischer, Claude, "The City and Political Psychology," *American Political Science Review* 69 (June 1975).

Flathman, Richard, *Political Obligation* (New York: Atheneum, 1972).

Frankena, William, *Ethics* (Englewood Cliffs, N. J.: Prentice-Hall, 1963).

Fredrickson, George, ed., *Neighborhood Control in the 1970's* (New York: Chandler, 1973).

Friedman, Milton, *Capitalism and Freedom* (Chicago: University of Chicago Press, 1962).

Friedmann, John, "A Response to Altshuler: Comprehensive Planning as a Process," *Journal of the American Institute of Planners* (August 1965).

Gay, Peter, *The Enlightenment: An Interpretation* (New York: Random House, 1966).

Glass, Ruth, "The Evaluation of Planning: Some Sociological Considerations," *International Social Science Journal* 11 (1959).
Goodman, Robert, *After the Planners* (New York: Touchstone Press, 1973).
Goodnow, Frank, *Politics and Administration* (New York: Russell & Russell, 1900).
Greenstone, J. David and Paul Peterson, *Race and Authority in Urban Politics* (Chicago: University of Chicago Press, 1976).
Gunnell, John, "Deduction, Explanation, and Social Scientific Inquiry," *American Political Science Review* 63 (December 1969).
Habermas, Jürgen, *Knowledge and Human Interests* (Boston: Beacon Press, 1971).
Hamilton, Alexander, James Madison, and John Jay, *The Federalist Papers* (New York: New American Library, 1961).
Hampden-Turner, Charles, *From Poverty to Dignity* (New York: Doubleday, 1974).
Hartman, Chester, et al., *Yerba Buena* (San Francisco: Glide Publications, 1974).
Harvey, David, *Social Justice and the City* (Baltimore: Johns Hopkins University Press, 1973).
Hawkins, Brett, *Politics and Urban Policies* (Indianapolis: Bobbs-Merrill, 1971).
Hegel, G. W. F., *The Philosophy of History* (New York: Dover, 1956).
Helvetius, Claude, *A Treatise on Man*, Vol. 1, (London: Albion Press, 1810).
Herson, Laurence J. R., "The Lost World of Municipal Government," *American Political Science Review* 51 (June 1975).
Hess, Karl, *Community Technology* (New York: Harper & Row, 1979).
Hill, Richard Child, "Fiscal Collapse and Political Struggle in Decaying Central Cities in the United States," in *Marxism and the Metropolis*, ed. by Tabb and Sawers.
Hobbes, Thomas, *Leviathan* (New York: Bobbs-Merrill, 1958).
Hofstadter, Richard, *The Age of Reform* (New York: Random House, no date).
Horkheimer, Max, *Critical Theory* (New York: Seabury Press, 1972).
Hume, David, *A Treatise of Human Nature* (Oxford: Clarendon Press, 1888).
Jenkin, Thomas P., *The Study of Political Theory* (Garden City, N. Y.: Doubleday, 1955).
Jennings, M. Kent, *Community Influentials: The Elites of Atlanta* (New York: Macmillan, 1964).
Kant, Immanuel, *Prolegomena to Any Future Metaphysics* (Indianapolis: Bobbs-Merrill, 1959).

Kant, Immanuel, *Foundations of the Metaphysics of Morals* (Indianapolis: Bobbs-Merrill, 1959).

Katznelson, Ira, *City Trenches* (Chicago: University of Chicago Press, 1981).

Keohane, Nannerl O., "Philosophy, Theory, Ideology," *Political Theory* 4 (February 1976).

Kershaw, Joseph, *Government against Poverty* (Chicago: Markham, 1970).

Klosterman, Richard E., "Foundations for Normative Planning," *Journal of the American Institute of Planners* (January 1978).

Kotler, Milton, *Neighborhood Government* (New York: Bobbs-Merrill, 1969).

Kramer, Ralph, *Participation of the Poor* (Englewood Cliffs, N. J.: Prentice-Hall, 1969).

Kristol, Irving, "Decentralization for What?" *The Public Interest* (Spring 1968).

Kuhn, Thomas, *The Structure of Scientific Revolutions* (Chicago: University of Chicago Press, 1970).

Laslett, Peter, ed., *Philosophy, Politics and Society* (Oxford: Basil Blackwell, 1956).

LeBreton, Preston and Dale Henning, *Planning Theory* (Englewood Cliffs, N. J.: Prentice-Hall, 1961).

Lewis, Oscar, *Tepoztlan: Village in Mexico* (New York: Holt, 1960).

Lichtheim, George, *The Concept of Ideology* (New York: Random House, 1967).

Locke, John, *The Second Treatise of Government* (New York: Library of Liberal Arts, 1956).

Loveridge, Ronald O., *City Managers in Legislative Politics* (Indianapolis: Bobbs-Merrill, 1971).

Lukács, George, *History and Class Consciousness* (Cambridge, Mass.: MIT Press, 1971).

Lupo, Alan, Frank Colcord, and Edmund Fowler, *Rites of Way: The Politics of Transportation in Boston and the U. S. City* (Boston: Little, Brown, 1971).

Macpherson, C. B., *The Political Theory of Possessive Individualism* (Oxford: Oxford University Press, 1962).

Mannheim, Karl, *Man and Society in an Age of Reconstruction* (New York: Harcourt, 1944).

Mannheim, Karl, *Ideology and Utopia* (New York: Harcourt, Brace & World, no date).

Marcuse, Herbert, *One-Dimensional Man* (Boston: Beacon Press, 1964).

Marris, Peter and Martin Rein, *Dilemmas of Social Reform* (New York: Atherton, 1967).

Marx, Karl, *Early Writings*, ed. by T. B. Bottomore (New York: McGraw-Hill, 1963).

Marx, Karl and Friedrich Engels, *The German Ideology* (New York: International Publishers, 1970).

McConnell, Grant, *Private Power and American Democracy* (New York: Random House, 1970).

McCoy, Charles and John Playford, eds., *Apolitical Politics* (New York: Crowell, 1967).

Melzer, Arthur, "Rousseau and the Problem of Bourgeois Society," *American Political Science Review* 74 (December 1980).

Michael, Donald, "Urban Policy in the Nationalized Society," *Journal of the American Institute of Planners* (November 1965).

Michael, Donald, *The Unprepared Society* (New York: Basic Books, 1968).

Miller, Eugene F., "Positivism, Historicism, and Political Inquiry," *American Political Science Review* 66 (September 1972).

Mollenkopf, John H., "The Postwar Politics of Urban Development," in *Marxism and the Metropolis*, ed. by Tabb and Sawers.

Morris, David and Karl Hess, *Neighborhood Power* (Boston: Beacon Press, 1975).

Moynihan, Daniel Patrick, *Maximum Feasible Misunderstanding* (New York: Free Press, 1969).

Mullins, Willard, "On the Concept of Ideology in Political Science," *American Political Science Review* 66 (June 1972).

Nisbet, Robert, *The Quest for Community* (Oxford: Oxford University Press, 1953).

Nordlinger, Eric, *Decentralizing the City* (Boston: Boston Urban Observatory, 1972).

Nozick, Robert, *Anarchy, State and Utopia* (New York: Basic Books, 1974).

Oakeshott, Michael, *On Human Conduct* (Oxford: Oxford University Press, 1975).

Oakeshott, Michael, *Rationalism in Politics* (London: Methuen, 1981).

Parrington, Vernon L., *Main Currents in American Thought*, Vol. 1 (New York: Harcourt, Brace & World, 1954).

Partridge, P. H., "Politics, Philosophy, Ideology," in *Political Philosophy*, ed. by Quinton.

Pateman, Carole, *The Problem of Political Obligation* (New York: Wiley, 1979).

Peterson, Paul, *City Limits* (Chicago: University of Chicago Press, 1981).

Plamenatz, John, "The Use of Political Theory," *Political Studies* 7 (1960).

Pocock, J. G. A., *The Machiavellian Moment* (Princeton: Princeton University Press, 1975).

Polsby, Nelson, *Community Power and Political Theory*, 2nd ed. (New Haven: Yale University Press, 1980).

Popper, Karl, *The Open Society and Its Enemies*, 2 vols. (Princeton: Princeton University Press, 1966).
Quinton, Anthony, *Political Philosophy* (Oxford: Oxford University Press, 1967).
Rousseau, Jean-Jacques, *The Social Contract and Discourses*, ed. by G. D. H. Cole (New York: E. P. Dutton, 1950).
Runciman, W. G., *Social Science and Political Theory* (Cambridge: Cambridge University Press, 1969).
Saint-Simon, Henri de, *Social Organization, The Science of Man, and Other Writings* (New York: Harper & Row, 1964).
Salkever, Stephen G., "Virtue, Obligation, and Politics," *American Political Science Review* 68 (March 1974).
Salkever, Stephen G., " 'Cool Reflection' and the Criticism of Values: Is, Ought, and Objectivity in Hume's Social Science," *American Political Science Review* 74 (March 1980).
Schiesel, Murray, *The Politics of Efficiency* (Berkeley: University of California Press, 1977).
Schutz, Alfred, *The Phenomenology of the Social World* (Evanston, Ill.: Northwestern University Press, 1967).
Shils, Edward, "The Concept and Function of Ideology," *International Encyclopedia of the Social Sciences*, Vol. 7.
Skinner, Quentin, "History and Ideology in the English Revolution," *Historical Journal* 8 (1965).
Skinner, Quentin, *The Foundations of Modern Political Thought*, 2 vols. (Cambridge: Cambridge University Press, 1978).
Smelser, Neil, *The Theory of Collective Behavior* (New York: Free Press, 1962).
Smith, Michael P., *The City and Social Theory* (New York: St. Martin's, 1979).
Sorel, Georges, *The Illusions of Progress* (Berkeley: University of California Press, 1969).
Steinberger, Peter J., "Hegel as a Social Scientist," *American Political Science Review* 71 (March 1977).
Steinberger, Peter J., "Social Context and Political Efficacy," *Sociology and Social Research* 65 (January 1981).
Steinberger, Peter J., "Political Participation and Communality: A Cultural/Interpersonal Approach," *Rural Sociology* 46 (Spring 1981).
Steinberger, Peter J., "Urban Politics and Communality," *Urban Affairs Quarterly* 20 (September 1984).
Stone, Clarence N., "Systemic Power in Community Decision Making," *American Political Science Review* 74 (December 1980).
Stone, Harold, Don Price, and Kathryn Stone, *City Manager Government in the United States* (Chicago: Social Science Research Council, 1940).

Strauss, Leo, "What Is Political Philosophy?" *Journal of Politics* 18 (August 1957).

Syed, Anwar, *The Political Theory of American Local Government* (New York: Random House, 1966).

Tabb, William K. and Larry Sawers, eds., *Marxism and the Metropolis* (New York: Oxford University Press, 1978).

Taylor, Charles, "Neutrality in Political Science," in *Philosophy, Politics, and Society*, 3rd Series, ed. by Peter Laslett and W. G. Runciman (Oxford: Basil Blackwell, 1969).

Thompson, Dennis, *The Democratic Citizen* (Cambridge: Cambridge University Press, 1970).

Toulmin, Stephen, *The Philosophy of Science* (New York: Harper & Row, 1963).

Vasu, Michael, *Politics and Planning* (Chapel Hill: University of North Carolina Press, 1979).

Walzer, Michael, *The Revolution of the Saints* (Cambridge: Harvard University Press, 1965).

Webber, Melvin, "Comprehensive Planning and Social Responsibility: Toward an A I P Consensus on the Profession's Roles and Purposes," *Journal of the American Institute of Planners* 29 (November 1963).

Weber, Max, " 'Objectivity' in Social Science and Social Policy," in E. Shils and H. Finch, eds., *Max Weber on the Methodology of the Social Sciences* (Glencoe, Ill.: Free Press, 1949).

Weber, Max, *From Max Weber*, ed. by Hans Gerth and C. W. Mills (New York: Oxford University Press, 1958).

White, Morton and Lucia White, *The Intellectual versus the City* (Toronto: New American Library, 1964).

Williams, Oliver, *Metropolitan Political Analysis* (New York: Free Press, 1971).

Wolff, Robert Paul, *In Defense of Anarchism* (New York: Harper & Row, 1976).

Wolfinger, Raymond and J. O. Field, "Political Ethos and the Structure of City Government," *American Political Science Review* 60 (June 1966).

Wolin, Sheldon, *Politics and Vision* (Boston: Little, Brown, 1960).

Yates, Douglas, *Neighborhood Democracy* (Lexington, Mass.: D. C. Heath, 1973).

Zimmerman, Joseph, *The Federated City* (New York: St. Martin's, 1972).

INDEX

Adams, John, 30
Adams, Henry, 71
Adorno, Theodore, 54
Adrian, Charles, 27
Advocacy planning, 44
Ahistoricity and human nature, 118–121, 127, 132
Alienation: and anarchism, 97; and communalism, 77, 81, 89–90; 92, 94, 134; and democracy, 67–68, 82; and the Enlightenment, 82–83, 85–87; and ethical theory, 92–94; and freedom, 82; meaning of, 81–83, 88–90
Althusser, Louis, 137
Altshuler, Alan, 39, 76, 77, 92
Anarchism, 96–98
Aristotle, 9, 12, 118, 136, 143, 149; on the nature of politics, 18; and the concept of citizenship, 141–142
Arkes, Hadley, 140–142, 146, 149
Atomization and human nature, 117, 119–121, 127, 132

Banfield, Edward, 4, 8, 115, 116, 130, 140; and political ethos theory, 32; account of urban crisis, 110–113; on atomization and ahistoricity, 119–120
Becker, Carl, 43
Behavioralism in political science, 2–7
Bellamy, Edward, 71
Bentham, Jeremy, 42, 52, 57
Bergson, Henri, 88
Berlin, Isaiah, 125
Bish, Robert, 24, 113–115, 119, 121, 130
Bodin, Jean, 12
Bureaucracy: and democracy, 39; growth of, 34; and managerialism, 61

Carmichael, Stokely, 75, 76, 77, 90, 92
Caro, Robert, 37
Castells, Manuel, 136–138, 142, 149
Childs, Richard S., 26
City planning. *See* Planning
Civic humanism, 98, 142
Civil service, 34
Cloward, Richard, 108
Commission plan. *See* Governmental structure
Community action: concept of, 63–66; criticisms of, 79; forms of, 66, 71–74
Community Action Program, 63, 65–66, 74, 91, 108–110
Community control, 23–24; and alienation, 92; distinguished from decentralization, 23, 68, 77–78
Community Development Corporations, 76, 77, 89, 91–92
Community power, study of, 4, 138, 146
Comte, Auguste, 42, 52, 57
Condorcet, Marquis de, 44, 45, 52, 57
Cooley, Thomas, 71–73, 147
Cotton, John, 30
Council-manager plan. *See* Governmental structure
Culture-of-poverty theory, 111–112, 119–120

Dagger, Richard, 141–142
Dahl, Robert, 4, 13
Davidoff, Paul, 52
Decentralization: distinguished from community control, 23, 68, 77–78
Democracy, 7, 70; and community action, 66–69, 76, 96–98, 99; and ethical theory, 96; and managerialism, 39, 69
Descartes, René, 47

Dewey, John, 73, 82–83
Diderot, Denis, 41
Dillon, John, 71–73
Dilthey, Wilhelm, 6
Durkheim, Emile, 81, 88

Economic analysis, 122, 125–126, 133–135; in Madison, 106–107; in neo-marxist approaches, 137–140; and possessive individualism, 103–104; and the study of urban politics, 113–115
Engels, Friedrich, 140
Enlightenment, the: and alienation, 82–83; and ethical theory, 50, 93–94; and freedom, 83; and the roots of managerialism, 41–47; 50–52, 83; view of science, 43
Equality, 145–147
Ethical theory and anarchism, 96–98; and communalism, 92–95, 109; and democracy, 96–98; in the Enlightenment, 50, 93–94; and human nature, 20; and managerialism, 49–50, 92–94; importance for political philosophy, 19–20; and positivism, 50; teleological and deontological, 55; and urban political philosophy, 132, 134–135, 140–142, 144, 146. *See also* Utilitarianism

Fact-value dichotomy, 51–52; critique of, 53–54, 56
Faludi, Andreas, 35
Federalism, 7–8, 24, 146; and the Cooley-Dillon controversy, 71–73; and political efficacy, 146–149
Feyerabend, Paul, 6
Ford Foundation, 63–65, 73–74

Fourier, Charles, 61
Freedom: and alienation, 82; concept of, 125; and managerialism, 62, 83
Friedman, Milton, 125, 140

George, Henry, 71
Gibbon, Edward, 41
Governmental structure: and behavioralism, 4; Commission Plan, 33; Council-manager Plan, 22, 26, 32–33, 56; and ideology, 129; metropolitan reform, 33, 114–115
Gray Areas Projects. *See* Ford Foundation

Habermas, Jürgen, 54
Hamilton, Alexander, 30, 107
Hamilton, Charles V., 75, 76, 77, 90, 92
Hampden-Turner, Charles, 76, 77, 78, 89–91
Harrington, James, 116
Harrington, Michael, 8
Hartman, Chester, 38
Hegel, G.W.F., 9, 14, 81, 94, 116, 144; and ahistoricity, 120; critique of Kantian ethics, 95; and the history of epistemology, 48; and the tradition of political thought, 10, 12
Helvetius, Claude, 41, 42, 50, 52, 61
Herder, J.G., 120
Herman, M. Justin, 38
Herrnstein, Richard, 110
Herson, Laurence J.R., 3–5
Hess, Karl, 91, 92
Hill, Richard Child, 138–139
Hobbes, Thomas, 12, 17, 19, 21, 121; on human rights, 123–126;

and state of nature theory,
116–118, 119
Horkheimer, Max, 54
Human nature: and alienation,
81–82; and ethical theory, 20–21,
141; managerialist conception of,
40, 41; and possessive-
individualism, 116–121, 127
Hume, David, 41, 47, 50–51, 120

Ideology: meaning of, 2, 8, 9–15,
21–22; distinguished from political philosophy, 24–25; 129–133,
135, 149–150
Invisible-hand arguments, 103, 106,
113, 115, 130

Jefferson, Thomas, 41
Jensen, Arthur, 110
Jouvenel, Bertrand de, 120

Kant, Immanuel, 19, 21, 94, 95,
140–141, 142; critique of
utilitarianism, 55–56; and
epistemological theory, 47–48
Keohane, Nannerl O., 10, 11
Kotler, Milton, 75, 91, 92, 115
Kristol, Irving, 79
Kuhn, Thomas, 6

Lenin, V.I., 140
Levellers, the, 116
Liberty, *See* Freedom
Locke, John, 12, 14, 101, 116; and
human rights, 124–126; on the
nature of the political, 143

Loveridge, Ronald O., 39
Lukács, George, 54, 81, 140

Machiavelli, Niccolo, 14
Macpherson, C.B., 116
Madison, James, 67, 105–108
Maistre, Joseph de, 88
Mannheim, Karl, 6, 52, 61
Marcuse, Herbert, 54, 81
Marx, Karl, 13, 81, 126, 141, 142,
149; and contemporary theories
of urbanism, 136–140; theory of
alienation, 88–89
Michael, Donald, 57–61
Mollenkopf, John H., 138
Morris, David, 91, 92
Moses, Robert, 37
Moynihan, Daniel Patrick, 8,
108–110, 115, 119–120, 130
Municipal reform, 22, 24, 26, 28, 31

Natural law: and communalism, 93;
and ethical theory, 144; in
Hobbes and Locke, 123–124; and
political obligation, 17
Neighborhood government, 23,
115, 130, 132, 133; and
democracy, 68, 75–77, 91–92; and
ethical theory, 94–95
Newton, Isaac, 43, 50
Nietzsche, Friedrich, 20, 88
Nisbet, Robert, 13, 61, 78, 81, 88
Nonpartisan ballot, 33
Nozick, Robert, 103, 121

Oakeshott, Michael, 49
Office of Economic Opportunity.
See War on Poverty

Ohlin, Lloyd, 108
Ostrom, Vincent, 24, 113–115, 119, 121, 130

Partridge, P.H., 9–10, 11
Plamenatz, John, 10
Planning: and community action, 79–80; conception of, 27, 35, 42; critique of, 38, 39; and municipal reform, 23; and science, 44. *See also* Advocacy planning
Plato, 9, 14, 17,19, 143; and political philosophy, 10, 12; on the purpose of politics, 18
Pluralism: 7, 143, 145–146; and democracy, 67; and managerialism, 39, 40, 134. *See also* Community power, study of
Policymaking, 144; and ideology, 129–130, 140; and managerialism, 29, 34, 37, 44, 61, 133; and Marxism, 138–139
Political obligation: communalist view of, 96–98; conception of, 16–17, 19; managerialist view of, 40, 59
Political philosophy, 24–25, 136, 149–150; nature of, 9–16, 18–19, 20–22; relationship to behavioralism, 3
Political theory, meaning of, 10
Politics and administration, distinction between, 37
Populism, 66, 73, 101
Positivism: critique of, 47,48; and the Enlightenment, 42, 50; and ethical theory, 50, 52
Poulantzas, Nicos, 137
Press, Charles, 27
Progress, 45–48, 57
Progressivism, 31–32; and planning, 27; and communalism, 73
Proudhon, P.-J., 88
Public choice theory, 113–114

Public interest: communalist view of, 100; managerial view of, 28, 39, 133; and possessive-individualism, 104–105, 107; Rousseau's theory of, 86
Public realm: communalist view of, 98; concept of, 17–18; managerialist view of, 40, 61

Race: and urban politics, 1, 7, 23, 128, 130; and community action, 75, 76, 79, 90; and culture-of-poverty theory, 111–112
Rawls, John, 20
Reform. *See* Municipal reform
Reiner, Thomas, 52
Rights, human, 100, 121–127
Rousseau, Jean-Jacques, 12, 96, 104, 116, 120; on autonomy, 94; theory of the General Will, 83–88; view of progress, 48–49

Sabine, George, 51
St. Augustine, 9, 12
St.-Simon, Henri de, 57, 61
St. Thomas, 12, 124
Sartre, Jean-Paul, 81
Schutz, Alfred, 6
Science, 45–48, 101, 132
Scientific management, 31
Settlement-house movement, 73
Smith, Adam, 104, 107
Social conflict, 79–80
Social science, 132; and natural science, 43, 44, 46, 48; and possessive-individualism, 101–102, 109, 112; and progress, 46, 58
Socrates, 17, 47
Sophocles, 17
Sorel, Georges, 49, 88
Special districts, 37

State of nature theory, 117–118, 121, 124
Stewardship, colonial concept of, 29
Strauss, Leo, 10
Sumner, William Graham, 71, 102
Syed, Anwar, 72

Taylor, Charles, 53, 54
Tocqueville, Alexis de, 61–62, 70, 72, 94, 147
Toulmin, Stephen, 6
Turgot, Anne Robert Jacques, 41
Tyranny: and communalism, 99, 112–113; and Madisonian democracy, 105–106

United States Constitution, 105, 147
Urban planning. *See* planning
Urban renewal, 63
Utilitarianism: critique of, 55, 93–94, 141; and freedom, 125; and managerialism, 69, 93; and the New England town, 70; and political obligation, 17; and positivism, 52; and possessive-individualism, 114

Vasu, Michael, 39

War on Poverty, and community action, 63, 65, 74, 91, 108–110
Webber, Melvin, 35, 46
Weber, Max, 6, 34, 53, 61
Williams, Roger, 69
Wilson, James, Q., 32
Wilson, Woodrow, 71
Wolff, Robert Paul, 96–97
Wolin, Sheldon, 61

Augsburg College
George Sverdrup Library
Minneapolis, MN 55454